Naked Being

Undressing Your Mind, Transforming Your Life

First published by O Books, 2010
O Books is an imprint of John Hunt Publishing Ltd., The Bothy, Deershot Lodge, Park Lane, Ropley,
Hants, SO24 0BE, UK
office1@o-books.net
www.o-books.net

Distribution in:

UK and Europe
Orca Book Services
orders@orcabookservices.co.uk
Tel: 01202 665432 Fax: 01202 666219
Int. code (44)

USA and Canada
NBN
custserv@nbnbooks.com
Tel: 1 800 462 6420 Fax: 1 800 338 4550

Australia and New Zealand
Brumby Books
sales@brumbybooks.com.au
Tel: 61 3 9761 5535 Fax: 61 3 9761 7095

Far East (offices in Singapore, Thailand,
Hong Kong, Taiwan)
Pansing Distribution Pte Ltd
kemal@pansing.com
Tel: 65 6319 9939 Fax: 65 6462 5761

South Africa
Stephan Phillips (pty) Ltd
Email: orders@stephanphillips.com
Tel: 27 21 4489839 Telefax: 27 21 4479879

Text copyright J. M. Harrison 2009

Design: Stuart Davies

ISBN: 978 1 84694 303 4

A CIP catalogue record for this book is available
from the British Library.

Printed in Great Britain by
CPI Antony Rowe, Chippenham, Wiltshire

O Books operates a distinctive and ethical publishing philosophy in
all areas of its business, from its global network of authors to
production and worldwide distribution.

Naked Being

Undressing Your Mind, Transforming Your Life

J. M. Harrison

BOOKS

Winchester, UK
Washington, USA

CONTENTS

To Margaret and David – Apples and Nanas.

Acknowledgements

A great big MERCI to my wife Wendy, and our children Holly and Georges for their patience, love and support.

Without you all – this book and this life would have been impossible.

L'amour est au-delà des mots et des mondes...

With endless love,

J xxx

A special thank you to Stephanie van den Bergh for her kindness and patience with the editing of this book.

A thank you to Beatrice and Laurence Stroud for their honesty, humour, humbleness and lifelong example.

Thanks to Sharon Jeffries for her years of unselfish, patient and considered listening.

My gratitude goes to Joe and Lyn Bowler for being themselves in *all* eventualities.

Namaste everyone.

Foreword

By Linda L. Panell – Creator and CEO of Conscious Alliances, Teleseminar Producer and Coach for the Evolution and Awakening of Consciousness

'*Mitakuye Oyasin*... All My Relations' is a Native American prayer that honours the connection, interconnection, and sacredness of all that is. It acknowledges the being-ness of our Earth and the Universe, and it reveals the ancient wisdom of oneness, wholeness and the power of who we are to touch all of creation with a thought, a breath, a whisper, or a heartbeat.

Chief Seattle understood this intricate, living web of connection. His words – ancient wisdom – touch modern hearts and souls:

> Man did not weave the web of life – he is merely a strand in it. Whatever he does to the web, he does to himself...

Modern science is now catching up with this ancient wisdom held by indigenous cultures who connected and communicated daily with the heart of the earth and the sky, allowing their own hearts to beat in sync with the planetary heart beat and their bodies to be as one with the rhythms and Laws of the Universe. Modern science now reveals that not only are we the strand within this web of life but also we are the web itself – a womb of unified consciousness, energy, and vibration. Every strand is the whole. Every thought sends vibrations to multiple universes awaiting with full attention to receive.

When I first heard this seemingly complex yet profoundly simple wisdom, I did not understand. In my upside down world, it made no sense to either my head or my brain, yet deep inside my heart, there was a deep knowing and an incessant gnawing to know more.

In my search for understanding and awareness, unfoldings became intense and frequent, yet only after I read Jonathan Harrison's first book, *We Are All One: A Call to Spiritual Uprising*, did I allow my brain to receive what my heart already knew. Jonathan's words were eloquent and easy. They touched that exquisite place of knowing deep within my soul, my spirit, and my heart because they came from that same space of knowing within him. They came from a depth of experience, not only intellectual awareness.

Over the past few years, my life has been a quest for awareness of both ancient wisdom and modern science. It has been an exploration of energy, vibration, and frequencies as well as their relationship to our oneness, our wholeness, and beyond.

In the beginning, my definition of wholeness was simple – 'Everything'. Nothing could work in isolation from all other things. Our businesses could not be separate from who we are in the bedroom; our passions could not exist only outside the office; we could not be creators and mothers and divas in one place and something else in our positions as leaders and friends. Our sexuality could not be separate from our spirituality. And my definition of 'Everything' was simple: mind, heart, body, spirit, finances, business, leadership, relationship, sexuality, nature, physical environment, and spirituality – a connection of separate parts.

Today, I am aware that our bodies, minds, and hearts are elegant and eloquent radio transmitters and receivers – the most sensitive ever created. They transmit and receive vibrations from the highest to the lowest measurable frequencies across the electromagnetic spectrum – frequencies beyond human comprehension, extending infinitely from and to the farthest reaches of the Universe. Everything is energy. Every single thought is energy. Every single emotion is energy. Each holds a vibration and a frequency that within milliseconds changes the Universe and all of creation around us.

Today, the word 'Everything' means so much more than a connection of separates. It contemplates conscious alliance with every other person in the world, with the collective connective consciousness, with every sentient being, with the sun, the moon, the stars, universes, multiple dimensions, galaxies, mother earth, all creation, all that ever was, all that ever will be, all the time – past, present, future. It contemplates the essential paradox that everything came from nothing, everything is nothing, and that nothing is all that is. It contemplates the convergence of ancient wisdom and modern science in ever-new, expanding, and evolving ways. Everything is everything else.

Within this convergence of ancient wisdom and modern science, authentic, raw Naked Being-ness emerges as the key to infinite possibility not only for humanity but for all of creation. And Jonathan Harrison's newest book, *Naked Being*, emerges as the authority.

This is a new era, a pivotal generation for creating a future of limitless possibility and pure potential for Planet Earth simply by remembering who we are – divinity: source Energy, pure creational power. The time is now to be the fullest expression of who we are – full out, full on, no withholds – freedom beyond measure. The time is now for Naked Being.

When we begin to remember who we are, we begin to align with and explore limitless possibility for wellbeing in spirit, body, mind, soul, heart, earth and beyond. We inspire others to remember and to BE their own fullest, most authentic expression. We break free from conditioning, old paradigms, rules, codes, fear and old stories. We rise together with one heart, one voice, one vibration in love to remember and re-create a vibrant New Earth for Her Children.

We understand our power to create any symphony and to choreograph any dance with and within this vast, majestic Universe using every vibration, every frequency, every nuance, combining them in multiple billions of patterns for creating new life – limitless possibility. We are both the creation and the creator of our lives. In this Universal Look Book™, we have an endless array of options from which to create. Nothing is withheld.

Naked Being holds the promise and the power to re-create our planet, making pollution, illness; terrorism, greed, and inequality disappear. It holds the possibility of healing the past, making gold from all the 'stories' we have spun into a million reasons to struggle, strive, endure, and suffer in pain. It holds all possibility for celebrating our children!

Now is the time!

We hold within our hearts all the creational power of the Universe.

According to Jonathan,

"The purpose of Naked Being is not personal gain, for your sense of ego dissolves into the reality of your True Nature. Naked Being manifests as a natural outward movement of compassion and protection for *all* living things. It is the acceptance of your natural place in the cosmic field of intelligence – the coming home to the realisation of what it means to be a human *Being*". (Naked Being #185)

Naked Being is true freedom – a breathtaking ride.

All my love,
Linda L. Pannell
www.consciousalliances.com
www.worldchangingwisdom.com
www.makelovetolife.com

Introduction

Believe nothing just because a so-called wise person said it
Believe nothing just because a belief is generally held
Believe nothing because it is said in ancient books
Believe nothing just because it is said to be of divine origin
Believe nothing just because someone else believes it
Believe only what you, yourself test and judge to be true.

Siddhārtha Gautama *aka* Buddha (563-483 BCE)

Naked Being is about coming home. Coming home to the formless heart of what you are. It doesn't involve adding to what you've already got, or acquiring something you don't yet have, simply the recognition and realisation of your true nature. That nature is not something you can be taught or anything you can learn to become. It is the simple truth of what you are – here and now in this very moment.

Reading this book is a journey in awareness. It's not *the* absolute route, or *the* only way, simply a collection of reflections to help guide you home. The further you travel down this sacred path of remembrance, the more you'll learn to discern and trust in your inner Self. For the True Self is the best navigation system in the entire universe. Not only does it help you understand *who* you are, but *where* you come from.

Nobody's saying this journey home is going to be easy. You'll need courage to face up to problems and difficulties, the honesty to deal with them and sufficient patience to see it all through. No one else can hold your hand or take this voyage of the soul for you, and yet at no time will you be alone, for you can *never* truly be alone.

You will know when you arrive home – not because you

logically understand it to be so, or because somebody tells you as much, but from the vibrant knowingness of love reverberating throughout your entire being. The joy you are is uncovered when the conditioning of the mind is withdrawn, for only then do you create enough space to truly 'see' yourself and reality as they are.

So these words are here to guide you, to comfort you and to help you question the meaning of life. They will make you happy and sad, laugh and cry, and if you allow them, they will move you as you need to be moved, for they contain the essence of what you are. If there is a 'purpose' for them, it is not personal gain, or to convince you of opinions, but to encourage spiritual momentum. They do not belong to a particular time, person or place, for they arose out of the timeless truth of Naked Being.

Approaching the nature of who you are means *allowing* your self to see more clearly, for allowance, acceptance and surrender are the three best revealers of that truth. The more you reveal or peel back from the outer layers of your being, the greater sense you will have of a formless underlying reality. You will increasingly see that people are neither what they appear to be, nor what they believe themselves to be; for beyond the physical, mental and emotional layers lies the foundational truth of Being, Naked Being.

All thoughts, theories, desires, concepts, ideas, experiences, memories, notions, emotions and appearances contribute to the conditioning or patterning of your mind. They define the way in which you think, speak and act. But *none* of these are the real you. They are only pale indications of a deeper essence. No name can define the realness of you, just as the colour of your hair or eyes do not substantiate who you are. Your body and looks are physical traits inherited from your parents. Even your name was given to a nameless you. When looking at yourself in the mirror, you are looking at *your* face, the face that belongs to you, which is an expression of you, but which does not and cannot substantiate the whole truth of who or what you actually are.

The same applies to your habitual mind. This separated ego-consciousness is not who you are, but something with which you identify. However, once you remove all the stories, notions, emotions and pent up baggage of the habitual mind, something happens. As it fades, an increasing space of clarity arises which allows you to see the bare truth of what you and reality are. For when that compulsive habitual mind is seen and stopped, the pure mind of universal consciousness is revealed. This is not something that belongs to you, but something everybody essentially *IS*. In short, pure mind is the most natural, transparent way of being.

In pure mind awareness, there is no reliance on the intellect to find an answer, just the effortless appearance of the solution. When you look at the world around you, the beauty of nature can be seen as that same pure mind in action. Surrender allows true expression. The acceptance of a sunflower is a stunning lesson if you only take the time to reflect upon it. This all makes further sense when you look up at the stars in the night sky and contemplate the ingenuity of the universe. For what genius could create and maintain such order and sustain such beauty and organisation? Like a drop of water in an endless ocean, the awareness of pure mind is a direct reflection of that same miracle.

Your True Nature can be considered 'Naked' – because it is the bare essence of what you are, and 'Being' – because it is unblemished existence. Now don't for one second think that this nakedness is embarrassing or leaves you in anyway vulnerable or exposed. The opposite is true. When you remember your Naked Being-ness, you experience a joyful relationship with your inner self, which leads to 'peace of mind' and a natural 'intelligent love' or compassion for all life. Your health will improve and your attitude to life will alter in the most positive ways. You will simply love being and naturally empathise with *all* forms of life. This essential nature or True Self is a treasure beyond your wildest dreams, and yet something so obvious it often remains overlooked. Being untouched and unaffected by time and space, we can't even say it 'exists' as such, and yet it underlies all.

We are human beings, but what do we know of the nature of Being? Truly knowing yourself means connecting with and remaining aware of your *whole* nature; remembering that you are limited (by form) and yet on the other hand limitless (through your relationship with formlessness). For only when you let go of what you appear to be, do you begin to sense what you truly are.

Naked Being is not a concept or a theory, neither is it a belief, religion or philosophy. It is the founding truth of our existence, the undisturbed nature of reality seen through the transparent unconditioned pure mind. It is the realisation of original peace, the experiencing of the clear blue sky of consciousness; and whether you realise it or not, it is the essence of what you are.

J.M.H – France 2009

Glossary of Terms

To quote the American author Mark Twain, 'Be careful reading health books. You may die of a misprint.' The descriptions and explanations herein are pointers to help guide you and not absolute definitions. Feel your way.

Duality: perceiving from subject to object. The partial view of reality seen by considering your 'self' to be separate from all 'else'. Form conscious of form.

Ego-self: the 'I' or 'me' illusory self which distinguishes from all others. Also known simply as self (lower case 's') or ego. Mistakenly thinks duality to be reality. Imagined being expressed through the habitual mind. A divided sense of reality accepted as complete and normal by the worldview (global) consciousness.

Fractionate State: a state of being in which the individual is cut off from their true nature and their own potential. As a consequence of this state of mind, people mistakenly seek to accumulate things, ideas, relationships, money or power in an attempt to find, create or sustain contentedness.

Habitual Mind: the conditioned state of mind keeping you out of reach of knowing your True Self. The home or 'host' of the ego, it is sustained and fed by its own sense of duality and separation.

Intelligent Love: spontaneous compassion without dependency on memory or emotion; one of the natural qualities of Naked Being. The universe itself is an expression of intelligent love in the form of life, order and beauty.

Joy of Being: the peace and harmony found to be present once the compulsions of the habitual mind are stilled. The 'bliss' YOU are.

Knowingness: the undoubted knowing of what is true without engaging conditioned logic and thought. The spontaneous recognition of reality.

Naked Being: your pure minded nature. The formless heart of what you are. You are a human being, but more precisely a human *getting to know* Being. When the layers or 'habits' covering your core nature are removed, you recognise the essential naked truth of pure consciousness that you and all others are.

Non-duality: the consciousness of non-separation, seeing no-subject and no-object. Non-duality (meaning not two) by name infers the opposite of duality.

Now: present moment awareness, as realised by the human mind once it is free of the bonds of the habitual mind.

Oneness: a non-dual realisation that all life is the ONE interconnected consciousness. When there is oneness, even the idea of 'being at one' is no longer present. There is just the inseparable present moment awareness of THIS.

Patterning: the personal, accumulated program of thoughts, emotions, memories instinctively used by the habitual mind. Your automatic mind program brought about by life circumstances and experiences.

Peace of Mind: another self-descriptive quality of Naked Being.

Pure Consciousness: The essential spirit nature of life. Consciously realised in the human being through the transparency of pure mind. Without it, nothing could be. The purpose of our existence is to recognise, realise and actualise this truth.

Pure Mind: the lens, window or mirror through, by or in which pure consciousness appears and is realised. As pure consciousness is light, pure mind is the mechanism through which that light is diffused.

Self: see True Self.

Self-knowledge: the undying knowingness that *all* versions of *self, you, reality, truth* etc are *ONE*. Truly knowing your S̲elf, you are inseparable from reality.

Soul: personified consciousness enabling learning, acting, feeling, living and loving your way back to the heart of Being. Personal, evolving and capable of being shaped and perfected. It is the traveller within.

Spatial Consciousness: perception of people and things from the subtle formless nature of inner space. Seeing and feeling the essential inherent beauty of Being.

THIS: profound non-personal awareness of pure consciousness. Not a dip in the ocean of oneness, but a merging with it. THIS is Life, Being, Self, conscious of itself.

True Nature: the way you are realised to be once the physical, emotional and mental layers of identity have been peeled back – your essential reality.

True Self: the absolute core of your being. As the ego expresses itself through the habitual mind, the True Self is the way of pure mind. Also denoted as Self with a capital 'S' as opposed to the little self of ego.

Truth: un-manipulated reality as it is. Unchangeable and everlasting. There are many truths, all leading to and from the one Truth.

Wholeness: the integration of consciousness into one overseeing awareness. The fusion of both the dual THAT (pointed to) and the non-dual THIS (the one living presence).

Worldview Consciousness: the current globally accepted manner of viewing ourselves, life and others which is constantly changing and evolving.

YOU: used to distinguish the transient 'you' of the habitual mind from the real YOU (pure consciousness). Your True Nature, the True Self, the essence of what you are.

Naked Being

1   Underneath everything you see, every thought you think and every emotion you feel, there is an essential dimension to life we all share. *This* is Naked Being.

o

2   Experiencing Naked Being takes place when you uncover the covered, for then you recognise that the Heart of what you are is not your body or your thoughts but pure consciousness itself.

o

3   'The energy of the mind is the essence of life.' Aristotle (384-322 BCE). All is consciousness. Continuing to identify with the little mind of ego *OR* your conscious surrender to reality is what defines your present awareness.

o

4   The garments or 'habits' you wear conceal the naked truth of your body by covering it with several layers. In the physical dimension, these clothes have a practical and beneficial purpose because they provide warmth, comfort and protection. Within the mind, layers of conditioned mental 'habits' actually *stop* you from experiencing Naked Being. They cover the pure mind with layer upon layer of conditioning, concealing your True Nature. This happens because you analyse and project from the egocentric habitual mind (the 'I, me, mine' way of thinking) in accor-

dance with your own personal patterning. This 'patterning' arises from a lifetime of conditioning. You could describe it as the 'route' taken by the individual mind which consequently determines your thoughts, words and actions. It is because of this patterning you are already deciding the meaning of what is presently occurring. You may also be deducing, proposing or imagining future alternatives, which all result in you overlooking the truth of the present moment. This is the habitual mind at work, the consciousness of separation you have grown accustomed to using. It sustains the belief that you are required to engage in conditioned thought in order to be you. But the truth is that you do not need to think or believe in order to be the awareness YOU are.

O

5   The mind becomes over-dressed by a masquerade of patterns and habits, for conditioned thoughts are not simply worn like clothes to cover and protect the body, but disguise the truth of who and what you are. As a direct consequence, these habits of mind change the way in which you 'see' reality.

O

6   Can you let go of your addiction to the ego-self that you and others have spent a lifetime inventing? For many in the world, this is too much to ask. To reveal that the 'life' you have built was constructed on unsuitable land with poor quality materials, and that one day it will all collapse, is a difficult reality to come to terms with. But beyond the mind of 'I', deep in the Heart of your being, is the only lasting reality you can truly realise – the True Self – your True Nature.

O

7   The constant noise of the habitual mind, like some annoying interference on an old fashioned radio, is gradually dissolved by tuning in to your inner Self. This is the recognition of Naked Being, revealed through a process of stripping back to what YOU already are, rather than acquiring more of what YOU are not.

O

8   Seeking comes in many forms – it begins with a fundamental purpose, and that purpose is often the seeking of personal benefit, fame, fortune, position and power. When these are discovered to be unfulfilling, then seeking takes another route.

O

9   Naked Being is not defined by intellect, wealth, status, colour, creed or religion. It is awakened in you through the discovery of inner being. You already have it within you; for it is what YOU are – you just need to be aware of its abiding presence.

O

10 Don't live your life thinking that the world owes you something. It's more that you owe the world the truth that YOU and the universe are inseparable. So pay it back. Be yourself. Your True Self.

O

11   Separation is sought and witnessed everywhere by the habitual mind because it is the mind of duality, the home of the ego-consciousness which is fed and sustained by difference. The ego-self looks outwardly, appearing as if you are *the* director recording *the* film of *the* life. That's because the habitual mind is so strongly identified with the idea of division that all else appears separate and 'otherly'.

O

12   By continuing to identify with the ego-self you are covering up reality. For attempting to see your True Nature with the habitual mind is like trying to look through a window which is covered with thick mud. Not until the window is cleaned and restored to its original transparency does everything appear clearly as it truly is. Sunlight cannot enter a room when the curtains are drawn.

O

13   The grasping way of the habitual mind means it is always seeking some label, state or condition, whether that be on an emotional, physical, or intellectual level. This is because it looks outwardly for 'things' it wants, which it believes can provide fulfilment. The fact is that when the habitual mind doesn't have these 'things' it leaves you feeling like a failure, unworthy or incapable of achieving happiness, and when it does have these 'things' the feeling of fulfilment comes and goes because the satisfaction is only fleeting. Before too long, you'll be off searching again, because this way of the mind cannot provide the permanent peace you know exists within YOU.

O

14   A 'fractionate state' results from the divided perception of the habitual mind. When in this state, you look for happiness outside of yourself. Believing you don't already have what it takes to be happy, you chase contentedness in identity, material things, emotions, relationships and other people. You are addicted to gathering temporary pleasures when all the time YOU are nothing less than perfectly happy. The habitual mind exists permanently within this *fractionate state* of consciousness. What is a fraction cannot realise wholeness on its own.

O

15   The self-addicted 'I, me, mine' nature of the ego cannot personally 'experience' Naked Being because it is present moment all-inclusive, non-personal awareness. In a sense there is no individual experience to be had, for you cannot recognize your non-dual essence unless you go beyond the ego's idea of its own uniqueness and separation.

O

16   The ego-self is both the judge and the jury. Each person it meets is rated and classified as better or worse, more or less. Smugly it suggests that they should have done this or that, or gloats over its own fortune and the misfortune of others. Everything and everybody is separate to it. The strength of the ego-self comes from discrimination, because it thrives on difference and division. Believing itself to be personally knowledgeable, it lacks Universal Wisdom.

O

17 Many of the stored details used by the habitual mind to decipher reality are linked to physical and emotional highs and lows. These remain consciously and sub-consciously glued to our understanding, thereby distorting our take on reality. So not only do thoughts get in the way, but pent up emotions and feelings too.

O

18 There exists an underlying, essential form of mind, which is primordial, clear and crystalline. This is pure mind. It is consciously recognised when habitual patterns and condi-tioning are stilled. Pure mind is like a transparent window which allows pure consciousness to shine through. By thinking of ourselves as separate we cut ourselves off from realising this natural flow of consciousness. It is not something mystical or supernatural but the most healthy and efficient way of the mind. *Everyone* has the possibility to realise pure mind.

O

19 Pure mind works because it is a transparent reflection of the universe from which you came, the way we realise our inherent relationship with pure consciousness. As the habitual flow of the mind drops away, the limitlessness of YOU appears.

O

20 The habitual mind is home to *your* habitual consciousness, as pure mind can be said to be the home to pure consciousness.

O

21   Nobody lacks pure mind, for it remains infinitely recognisable, while continuing to be overlooked. Accepting the possibility of pure mind is the beginning of transformation and change. For if we accept its existence, we begin to remove our own 'personal layers' which disguise its permanent presence. Does it exist? Take a look...

O

22   Where is your mind? Your habitual mind believes it exists somewhere in the centre of *your* head. In this respect it appears to be yours, something confined and limited to you. That's why it's something *you think* you are and not the founding truth of *what* you are. When you begin to *feel* what YOU are, pure consciousness is seen everywhere.

O

23   From the standpoint of the habitual mind, the pure mind of Naked Being appears impossible, too simple and too good to be true.

O

24   Experiencing Naked Being 24/7 is the nature of peace, the true meaning of freedom and the way home for us all.

O

25   You have an opportunity to approach the truth of Naked Being right here, right now. You don't have to wait. For who is waiting? Why are they waiting? What are they

waiting for? For that truth is what you presently are. It exists inside you, a flame which can never be removed or extinguished – only obscured, postponing your recognition further still. For beneath this personal plethora of mind-body memorised details and habits, there abides an eternal sacred Heart.

O

26   How then can you approach Naked Being? It is not something you need to look outside yourself for, for it is already here. It is what YOU are. So the answer lies in removing the layers which disguise it. Having an open mind is the first step towards experiencing your True Nature. Allowing old ideas of what reality is – to be put aside. This may not be easy, for since childhood the idea of what you are has been based upon identifying with your name, age, career, looks, feelings or even emotions. Yet none of these details define what YOU are, for they are all patterned conditions you memorise, experience or share. They are transient, they change and come and go, whereas YOU are *always* here, for YOU are the underlying awareness presently reading these words.

O

27   Open your mind to the possibility that at the core of your being you are not separate. That separation alone could just be an outer illusion and in reality you and everybody else are individual expressions of a greater whole. The conditioned you is not the whole story, just a camouflaged appearance. Your True Self doesn't need to be seen or thought of as any-thing. For what YOU are is already perfect. What YOU are is the Truth, but you cannot see it

yet because you have been conditioned to look outwardly and not inwardly towards your formless unbounded nature.

O

28   Opening up to the possibility that you are not so separate, then you must also see that the need for you to pass judgement or to see another person as inferior or superior is a pointless exercise. The idea of absolute difference between yourself and another can only arise if you continue to discriminate, otherwise you must be equal. Not identical, but equal. Individual in expression of form and character but having the same essence as *any* other.

O

29   Naked Being reveals that everyone's a teacher and every moment a lesson. You, your partner, friends and children, even those we never meet are all teachers and guides. For example, who do you think taught us more in the last century – Ghandi or Hitler? Ghandi was a conscious teacher who expounded an increasingly pure teaching. Hitler on the other hand can be said to have taught us greatly through his own ignorance and was therefore an ignorant teacher. They can both be considered our teachers, for knowingly or unknowingly they provided the same lessons and signposts for humanity. In the end, Hitler taught us compassion through his heinous actions and Ghandi taught us compassion through his example of non-resistance and unity.

O

30   There are no superior or inferior beings; there is just Being appearing in a multitude of forms, all moving towards the recognition of their ONE essence.

O

31   When you pursue the core of ego-self, its influence becomes withdrawn. It cannot continue to dominate your consciousness once it is recognised for what it is – a conglomeration of thoughts. But be grateful for this sense of ego, for it is the seeking mechanism which allows you to uncover your True Nature. Use the ego to seek inner truth, for then it will be enveloped by the peace and love YOU are.

O

32   The ego-self of the habitual mind primarily focuses on becoming, and as a consequence, constantly overlooks the reality of the present moment. It also concerns itself with wanting to have, which again arises from the mistaken idea that you will find lasting fulfilment sometime, somewhere in the future. There is only one true lasting joy – and that is present here and now. It can never *be* anywhere else. It can never be *found* anywhere else. It is the Joy of Being, the joy of knowing and being YOU.

O

33   Naked Being is something we seek and yet something we already are.

O

34   Without awakening to Naked Being you will continue to feel a sense of incompletion in your life. This is because partial knowledge of what you are can only provide a fleeting glimpse of peace. The real peace you yearn for is an everlasting peace, intuitively known to exist somewhere in the depths of your being.

O

35   'In the sky there is no distinction of east and west; people create distinctions out of their own minds and then believe them to be true.' This quote from Siddhārtha Gautama, *aka* Buddha (563-483 BCE), shows the way in which the habitual mind works. Ironically, it slices up the whole in an attempt to define what that whole is. This dualistic caveman-like way of obtaining knowledge through the senses provides a necessary understanding of the layers of form. But it mutates reality because it ignores the contribution of formlessness in the realisation of the whole. If we understand that the habitual mind is made up of layer upon layer of this type of mental, genetic, social and political conditioning, then we can understand that the universal truth of what we are is only bared once all these layers or habits are removed.

O

36   'To see a world in a grain of sand – And heaven in a wild flower – Hold infinity in the palm of your hand – And eternity in an hour.' William Blake (1757-1827 CE) from *Auguries of Innocence*. Life's a beach! The habitual mind, relying on its own fragmented version of life, assumes that in order to grasp the reality of a sandy beach it has to systematically count and examine *each* grain of sand –

which of course it can never do. Pure mind on the other hand is aware that going inside one grain reveals the entire nature of the whole beach. The grain *is* the beach – for the beach is in the grain.

O

37 Of course doubts will continue as your ego-self begins to struggle. Your ego will suggest that you don't really need to adapt, that there is something to fear in change and anyhow you are 'alright jack'. Perhaps you will continue to mislead yourself with the notion that you are special, that you are something more or better than others. Or the low self-esteem proposed by the same habitual mind will sustain the thought that you are less worthy than others and undeserving. In both cases the fear of letting go of the ego's identity is what gets in the way.

O

38 All you see as reality is caused by your mind's patterning. But what is undeniable to everyone is the awareness of existing. You know you exist. As a little exercise to study this, without touching or resting on anything hold one of your hands out in front of you. Keep it as still as you can. Study your hand. Sense that you are not your hand, because you are looking at your hand. Simply by looking deeply at that hand, you can sense the aliveness, the vibrant life force energy which flows within and around it. However, your hand is unable to study you, because it is something which *belongs* to you and not what YOU are. It exists as a part of your material body. If that same hand was removed due to an accident, you would still exist where you are, with one hand instead of two, but never-

theless with the same awareness. This means you are not *just* your body. The physical body is a layer of being, an overcoat of matter. So is the true you to be found in the habitual mind of the ego-self? The fact that you have the ability and freewill to change your habitual mind means that it cannot be the real you, otherwise YOU would be a very worrying collection of many minds by now! The truth is that YOU never change. *Never* has and *never* will. Only the awareness of what YOU are alters.

O

39   By observing your thoughts, you begin to realise they are not you. Thoughts arise in the mind through a process which you can learn to observe. The Naked Being YOU are exists *underneath* the thought, which becomes obvious when you watch a desire arising and deliberately choose to alter its course or stop it developing. In essence YOU are what the early Gnostics called forethought. This is because you are not simply your body. YOU are not just your habitual mind or your thoughts and emotions. YOU are the reality before the thought. YOU are Spirit. YOU are peace. YOU are intelligent love. YOU are a window through which pure consciousness recognises itself. Like all forms of life you are in the process of discovering your true relationship with Being.

O

40   Opening your mind to the possibility of growth and trans-formation means taking a step back from running on the automatic gears of the ego-self. To allow space in your consciousness to appear before leaping in with the same old predictable thoughts of the past. The patterning of the

mind follows your habitual 'program', but the truth is that there is a natural universal 'program' already running which needs no updating and requires no downloading because it is already perfectly present within you. The only obstacle to this is your ego-self which acts like a computer virus increasingly reducing your natural ability to operate efficiently. Using the program of the habitual mind is akin to installing 'malicious' software you don't realise to be harmful, but which eventually leads to the computer malfunctioning or crashing. Taking a step back from your computer-like thought process creates a space in which you can observe what's really going on.

O

41   By reversing your attention you can become aware of the sound of silence. For instance, as I listen to my two children playing outside in the garden, instead of simply listening to their shrieks of excitement, I can learn to become aware of the silent gaps between their joyful outbursts. This silence is always there. It never leaves. All sounds emerge from that silence and without that silence there would be no expression. It is the same with pure consciousness. It is here, now, always, and everything comes through and out of it. Wherever you are, contemplation of the sound of silence is something you can practice on a daily basis.

O

42   The true meaning of 'being present' arises when you are wholly and unconditionally aware of your aliveness in the present moment. For then it is Naked Being that is consciously present – and not any separate sense of 'I'.

O

43   There is nothing for you to do, for you are already Naked Being – and you can never be separated from yourself. However, there is much to *stop* doing. Stop fearing; stop seeking, stop thinking, stop worrying, stop looking and stop doubting.

O

44   Don't try to imagine what will happen, for ego-based projections of the future invariably end in anxiety and turmoil. You are already creating your future. What you are thinking now, in this very moment, is the key to what the future holds for you.

O

45   So you already have within you all you need, just remove what lies in your way. There's nothing to grasp, learn, attain or master, just everything to simplify.

O

46   Frustration only arises because things don't turn out as the habitual mind hoped. The cause of the frustration is not the event itself, but the attitude of the hoper. So who is the hoper? The ego-self. When you surrender to what is, the hoper dissolves. Reality has no versions or alternatives, it just IS.

O

47   Begin by forgiving and baring yourself, by laying open all

the thoughts, words and deeds which have accompanied you on your travels and seeking something better you intuitively know to exist. Be open with yourself, and then you will find yourself open to growth and change.

O

48   Shockingly, you access Naked Being by not thinking. By not relying on the idea that you need to continuously conclude, define and interpret everything. Does the sun 'think' where to shine its light? When all your 'personal layers' fall away, so will any idea of a separate self. The ego-self appears to be what you are, when it is just a tiny mistaken reflection.

O

49   Stop your thoughts and experience the peace and Joy of Being, for that is where you came from, that is where you are and that is where you will always be. That permanent peace and everlasting joy appears when you look and listen without mental commentary. For when the habitual mind is stilled, the pristine awareness of what you are can be directly experienced.

O

50   Now you may be concerned that by stopping your thoughts you will lose the ability to be you. But rest assured that you lose nothing – in fact, you only gain increasing clarity of what it is that YOU are. You are focusing your attention on the present moment – the Now. In this way you apply your fullest presence to the task in hand whatever that may be, so that even sweeping the

floor can provide the opportunity for you to make a powerful connection with the universe. Then even taking the seemingly monotonous trip to work becomes an 'open to all possibilities' spiritual experience. You may even find yourself running to catch the train, but underneath all this chaotic exterior appearance you continue to recognise the ever-present awareness YOU are. You cannot ever be separate from the pure mind nature YOU are, even though thoughts and appearances suggest otherwise. There is no need to change the understanding of who or what YOU are in order to run for the train, although it might well involve the mind asking the legs to run! When you are truly present, you will act according to the demands of each situation. So accept that each element of your being has a specific job which it is created to do. Your ears for listening, your taste buds for tasting. After all, you wouldn't use your toe to cough would you? Release what is required of you in any given moment. Life happens, and Naked Being was there before, during and after *any* turn of events. It cannot go away because unlike the train, it never arrived. It is just here and always here. Once you recognise the permanent presence of Naked Being, it will be seen to underlie whatever you do because it can never be taken away. For unaware or aware, you are always YOU.

O

51   If you can stop *all* thoughts from arising *and still remain conscious and alert*, then it is possible to recognise that without any thought coming into your head you are still here, still present. So what you are must be something other than your thoughts – you must be *the awareness itself.*

O

52   Most human beings are selfish (they want for themselves), impatient (they want it right away), greedy (they want more) and lacking in focus, for their focus is desire and wanting, which of course they can never have, because they will always imagine something else they want next.

O

53   You can own everything – but if you fail to recognise your True Nature, then you have nothing of real value.

O

54   Lasting peace of mind cannot be found outwardly. At times you may feel deliriously happy or temporarily satisfied, but never at permanent peace. Personal expectations will occasionally be exceeded or failed to be met at other times. Hopes and dreams will come and go. For the fullness of life is recognised when you recognise that YOU are not found through chasing the desires of the habitual mind, but from surrendering to the timeless presence of Naked Being.

O

55   Wanting to possess things, people, memories or feelings is based on the mindset that we can receive lasting happiness from them. However, that wanting remains unsatisfied even when we succeed in getting those objects of our desire. Whatever form our desire takes, what we are really trying to attain is the permanent peace and contentedness of our True Nature.

O

56   What is not real comes and goes. Naked Being has nowhere to go, nothing to do and no time in which to do it.

O

57   When you choose to remember Naked Being, you are welcomed home like a long lost friend. When you ignore its reality, you cannot fully understand what is missing in your life.

O

58   When you initially touch pure mind, you may experience oneness – the essential interconnectedness of all things. From that first meeting onwards, life itself is seen as a 'way' – a way home.

O

59   Underneath your body is your habitual mind. This is what you think you are most of the time. But underneath *your* body and underneath that mind – you are the free boundless universe.

O

60   Naked Being is not a transient quality, but an eternal reality. Instinctively and intuitively follow life like a sunflower follows the radiance of the sun, for then you will meet, greet and embrace your True Nature.

o

61   The True Self is camouflaged by the activity of the ego-self. Conditioned habits act like layers of ignorance disguising the power, presence and value of inner wisdom. The habitual mind only remains in control as long as you continue to identify with it.

o

62   Diminish the presence of the ego-self by looking directly at it. The more regularly the thoughts of the ego are recognised and noticed, the easier it is to see through the habitual mind's false projected version of reality. When you laugh at yourself you know you are growing. If you laugh at yourself too much, then see a shrink!

o

63   When you have ended the wild goose chases of the ego-self, then you awaken to peace of mind and intelligent love. This pure mind is unquestionably known to be what YOU are, not through conditioned logic, but through a knowingness which goes beyond the senses.

o

64   If you want to see the truth of what you are, then empty your mind and give the stillness that remains your undivided attention.

o

65   Naked Being is an evolutionary step for humanity. For

should this become the foundation of the accepted worldview consciousness, then the primitive ignorance which continuously manufactures war will come to an end, illness will be increasingly overcome, and birth and death will be realised to be part of the ONE inseparable LIFE.

O

66   The ladder of human evolution leads us through three stages. Recognizing what we are, realising what we are capable of, and putting our potentials into action. These three stages of growth are critical to the development of our species. They are also the stepping stones for discovering and implementing your True Nature.

O

67   There is no struggle required to become free. YOU are free. However, your present awareness of that freedom remains restricted by the belief that you are absolutely separate.

O

68   The habitual mind perceives reality through the world of form. So when you transcend the ego-self, you transcend the limitations of the world of form.

O

69   The mind-body perspective is bound by time and space. Naked Being is free of these restrictions. For Truth is both timeless and limitless, beyond any conceptual boundaries

or limits created by the human mind.

O

70   It is not just the past that holds power over you, but also the future. Thoughts of doubt, as well as hopes and fears arise through your 'guestimations' of what will be. To end this speculation, simply *stop* guessing and *stop* gambling with what will or will not happen in your life. If you can learn to no longer depend on the past *or* the future, then you will remain connected to the present moment. For the past is gone (it doesn't exist) the future has not arrived (it doesn't exist) and yet the present (reality) is here and now.

O

71   The old habitual view of what you are gradually falls away. It may not completely fade from your memory, but is no longer the central focus, for you realise it to be detrimental to the health, happiness and well-being of yourself and others.

O

72   Pure mind expresses the consciousness of the universe. In this sense it is both within you and outside of you. Like the apparently infinite stars it manifests in millions of different ways, but its essence remains ONE.

O

73   'We are shaped by our thoughts; we become what we think. When the mind is pure, joy follows like a shadow that never leaves.' Siddhārtha Gautama (Buddha). YOU

are already that pure mind, just let go of the habitual patterns which stand in the way.

O

74 The essential truth of what you are is discovered through experiencing pure mind. As Naked Being is uncovered, the separation of subject and object fades, and the old you melts into oneness, revealing that everything and everybody emanates from a single essence.

O

75 Life is seen by the habitual mind to be diverse and many, but realised by pure mind to be ONE.

O

76 In realising Naked Being all you see is the oneness of the True Self. Indivisible, it remains unchanged by thoughts, intellectual concepts, memories or emotions.

O

77 Loneliness is an illusion of the habitual mind. How can you be lonely when YOU are inseparable from the universe?

O

78 The ego-self thrives on separation but seeks to be whole. Pure mind doesn't seek and can never be divided. So which can provide peace?

O

79   Within Naked Being the outdated perceptions of the habitual mind fall away. Personal needs and desires no longer dominate the flow of consciousness. All the accumulated knowledge of the habitual mind pales into insignificance. Knowledge for the self feeds the ego, but Self-knowledge is wisdom which humbles the soul.

O

80   The ego will propose a thousand ways in which it is special and different, but none can or will last. Once the dominance of the ego is withdrawn, oneness is neither hard nor easy, simply what *IS*.

O

81   YOU are realised through emptying the mind of all notions of separation and self. Mind is still there but in its untouched, unblemished state. Therefore Naked Being is not a state of 'no-mind', but the transparent or pure mind best able to reflect the essential basis for LIFE.

O

82   Mind and thought are not one. After all, when a glass (the mind) is emptied of water (habitual patterns and thoughts), it is still a glass (mind), but now an empty glass which is full of air (pure).

O

83   Present moment awareness arises from the way in which

you use your mind, for consciousness holds the key to being. Using your mind simply, openly and naturally, you will see in a way the intellect cannot. This is because you will have emptied yourself sufficiently to realise the presence of LIFE itself.

O

84   Contented, kind and forgiving, loving and affectionate and always ready to lend a hand to those in need. These are not characteristics of a perfected individual – but the ordinary communal nature of Naked Being.

O

85   The way to measure where you presently are in realising Truth is to see how efficient you are at removing the obstacles in its way. For how often do you need to be reminded that YOU are what you are looking for?

O

86   Truth is not reached by *doing* something but *being* what you are. So let go of the idea that you need to find, do or attain something. You can never be anything else other than the True Self. You can only pretend to yourself and others it is otherwise.

O

87   If you think you exist without the True Self, who is behind that thought? It is the schismatic nature of the ego seeking to cling to the illusion of separation.

O

88   When the ego-self is subdued, having to think is replaced by the transparent awareness of Naked Being. This is cosmic intelligence shining luminously through the window of pure mind. It needs no thought, no idea, for it naturally unfolds in an intelligent, loving and positive way.

O

89   What you *think* you are will change. What you *really* are will not – and the gap between the two will narrow in time.

O

90   The real miracle of life appears when you set yourself free from the patterns of your mind. Free from all conditions – you are that miracle.

O

91   Many hold back from the reality of Naked Being because it overrides the superficial sense of their ego.

O

92   'To be full of things is to be empty of God. To be empty of things is to be full of God.' Meister Eckhart (c.1260-1328 CE). So what are these 'things' which need to be emptied from our minds? They are nothing less than our habitual identities, emotions, images and thoughts. They bring you to the conclusion that everything exists outside of you

—when in reality *all is within*.

O

93   With the habitual mind silent and still, the emptiness of pure mind is uncovered. The natural fullness of that uncluttered space is undeniable. How ironic it is that when you let go of the habitual mind, you discover that you are already full – full of emptiness. An emptiness so alive you can feel it resounding through every part of your being. This is the reunion you have been waiting for since the error of time began, because you have come home. Limitlessness itself opens up because you are now in tune with the boundless loving nature of pure mind. You feel an unrivalled compassion for *all* life, which is no longer linked to emotion, for it is the presence of intelligent love – the love unconditioned by desire or emotion. It cannot separate itself from anything, for it is knowingly present in all. Unable to discriminate, it manifests in the best interests of *the whole*.

O

94   Grace is not something you can be given, not a special reward bestowed by a divine being, but the natural process through which your True Nature (YOU) is revealed.

O

95   Reality is found in the gap, the silence, the space between thought. You do not need to think in order to exist, but you need to exist in order to think. Awareness, not thought, is the core of what you are, whether confined to

a body or not. The quickest way to become conscious of that is to remove all the things which stand in your way. Find inner space and spend time dwelling within it. This means to develop spatial consciousness.

O

96 The reality is that you have more in common with space than you know, for you are 99.9 per cent space, so you have more of a connection with this 'nothingness' than you perhaps realise. And like you, that so called 'empty space' is inseparable from pure consciousness.

O

97 Developing spatial consciousness requires the shifting of awareness from form to formlessness, from outer to inner, by becoming mindful of space. Rather than the habitual 'seeing is believing', spatial consciousness is more like 'feeling the being-ness' by first engaging, and then going beyond the senses. In this way you wholeheartedly taste reality, rather than relying on preconceived ideas, labels, notions or memories of how something should be.

O

98 Perception begins with the senses. Then your mind's habitual patterning translates the information provided by the senses. YOU remain the nameless, faceless witness underlying both. Without habitual patterns obstructing your mind, the pure nature YOU are consciously appears.

O

99   Contemplate the spaces or gaps which arise between your thoughts. The thoughts come and go and yet YOU are always here. When you continue to be mindful of this process, the silent pauses will lengthen and deepen. Keep practising this on a daily basis and like a muscle, your spatial consciousness will develop.

O

100   There are many ways to acknowledge space in our lives. There is the space between thoughts, the space found in silence, the space between the breaths, the space found in nature or the space in which the stars of the cosmos appear. Before reacting – in thought, word or deed – allow a space or gap to arise. By doing this you are providing a way to introduce more clarity into your life, providing a direct connection with Being.

O

101   Blending with nature allows you to experience that life springs from the ONE source. Experiencing the true reality of anything or anyone requires the habitual mind to stop or step out of the way, for only then is the ONE essence uncovered and engaged.

O

102   Observing nature is a way to reveal Being-ness. For example, the oak tree outside my window can be viewed from a dual perspective. I am *here* and the tree is *there* – for I am looking at *the tree*. This is the separation and difference proposed by habitual mind. However, when the tree is mindfully engaged without inner commentary,

then something else happens. Through spatial consciousness, a new dimension awakens as I begin to 'sense' the real being or essence of the tree. As this exchange deepens, the tree and any sense of 'I' become fused together. The two become one. Duality dissolves into non-duality. 'I' and the tree are inseparable. This is the surfacing of pure mind.

O

103   Another oak tree in the garden is about one hundred years old. It stands tall and strong, yet slightly leaning to one side. From a deeper perspective it is recognised to be doubtless, fearless and true. There are points in the trunk where it bends this way or that, places where more leaves appear on some of the branches than others and sporadic gaping holes where parts of the tree have been completely snapped off during powerful storms. Large areas of the bark are covered with green and aquamarine coloured moss and lichen. You could never say that it was physically perfect – and yet in this moment it is perfectly imperfect. Just like you.

O

104   If there is a continued 'effort' to re-establish a 'higher' consciousness or altered state then the duality of the seeker and the sought still exists, for 'someone' remains divided from 'something' else. But what and why? In all these cases the habitual mind is returning to the idea of separation, when in reality you are never divided from the wholeness YOU are. YOU are what you seek. So what steps are you taking to narrow that gap?

O

105 The problem with habitual thinking is that it dissects reality. What is already whole doesn't need cutting up and labelling, just accepting and appreciating *as it is*. The isolated consciousness of the ego-self separates you from the truth of what YOU are

.

O

106 Only *you* can find the truth of what YOU are. Along the way you may need to develop specific practices, the help and comfort of a particular system, the benefits of a certain school of thought, the support of an ancient belief, or the words of a Guru. Depend on these as long as you need, for in the end they all point to the YOU reading this sentence.

O

107 Be mindful of your weaknesses as well as your successes. Practice what you need to practice, learn what you need to learn and above all remain honest with yourself. Then you will continue growing. If you believe that you have no growing left to do, then your ego has lulled you into a false sense of security.

O

108 One of the purposes of meditation is to prepare sufficient 'space' for pure mind awareness. When all voices, visions, lights, music, colours and similar emanations of the habitual mind have finished, you are eventually left with nothing but a blank screen from which there is no desire

or need to deviate from. Developing mindful awareness or
'mindfulness' of that 'nothing' leads to Naked Being.

O

109   Through meditation you may experience a deep sense of
        peace by disengaging the habitual mind. However, if that
        peace *only* occurs when your eyes are closed, then it
        remains something separate from the world. The peace
        found at the heart of meditation underlies every moment
        of your life, but you don't always see it. So return that
        sense of love and well-being to where it is most needed –
        open your eyes – and bring it back into the world.

O

110   The purpose of spiritual practice is to prepare the habitual
        mind to accept the reality of the Self. You choose a method
        according to your understanding, but a time arises when
        all practices can be let go. For when you ask yourself *who*
        is practicing *what,* you realise the existing separation
        between the two. You are somebody going through a
        process of tasting some 'other' version of reality, when the
        ONE true reality is undeniably here *all the time.*

O

111   Your essential being is pure consciousness. To realise that
        Self doesn't mean finding something 'else', but giving up
        what it is not. When everything that is not YOU is relin-
        quished – then only what YOU are remains.

O

112   There are three aspects to everyone's identity or *tridentity*. Firstly, what they *appear* to be. Secondly, what they *think* they are (patterning of emotions, intellect, stories and sub-conscious baggage) and thirdly, the unblemished *essential truth* of *what* they are. Your body *appears* to be you. Your habitual mind *thinks* it's you. Pure consciousness *is* YOU.

O

113   YOU are enlightened awareness. How difficult is this to see? About as difficult as seeing the nose on your face without looking in the mirror. It's here and now, but unless you realise how and where to look, you just won't see it.

O

114   Imagine your True Self sitting in the middle of a bright, white room on a large comfy cushion. The experiences of life enter that room in the shape of forms, names, labels, thoughts, emotions and haphazard occurrences. The True Self accepts all these things, welcomes them and allows them to take place without becoming identified or entangled with them. They are observed arriving, allowed to be expressed and seen to leave by the open window, for they are realised to be simply the comings and goings of existence. The True Self remains unchanged. On the other hand the ego personally identifies with these illusions through misjudgement, compulsion and comparison creating untold mental, emotional and physical debris. Time and effort is then required to clean the mess away. So the choice is yours. Untidy or clear. Complication or clarity. Illusion or Truth.

O

115   To believe that *your* mind is the pinnacle of existence is ignorance. Was it *your* mind which created the world? To think that *you are* the universe is yet another form of ignorance. Pure consciousness is not yours alone, but the ONE loving intelligent flow of the energy of LIFE that YOU both share and are.

O

116   The habitual mind cannot see your True Nature, for when the Self is knowingly present, the habitual is decidedly absent.

O

117   Worries and doubts occur because of the concept of time, which arises in the time bound consciousness of the habitual mind. Pure mind is the timeless Now, where there is no space for mental stress.

O

118   Suffering arises from habitual conditioning. Pure mind is unconditioned. So what does this signify?

O

119   Knowledge hoarded for personal gain is a vain selfish belonging, but Self-knowledge shared for the benefit of all is Universal Wisdom.

O

120   Truth is everywhere, but only *found* within. It may be spoken, but never thought.

O

121   Your habitual mind struggles to imagine an answer for every question, but it cannot answer the question of its own identity. Stuck in its own divided version of reality, it has no permanent foundation in truth itself. It cannot define its own being. It exists temporarily because it has evolved via thought – a mirage the mind has imagined into existence. What has been created will pass away. What was never created always remains. Behind the thought of what you are, lies the permanent unchanging truth of YOU.

O

122   Pure mind, knowing itself, knows everything needed to be known.

O

123   'When you strip and are not embarrassed, and you take your clothes and throw them down under your feet like little children and trample them, then you will see the Child of the Living One and you will not be afraid.' *Jesus of Nazareth*, extract from *The Gospel of Thomas*. This quotation from the Nag Hammadi texts provides another example of Naked Being. The 'clothes' Jesus refers to here represent the layers of conditioning which disguise your pure minded nature. Only when you let go of your mind-body identity do you awaken to the truth of what YOU are. Naked Being is the raw, unabridged truth, unable to be monopolised or separated. It is what you were, are and

will always be.

O

124 Freedom is an aspect of Truth. Anything which denies freedom is not based on truth but ignorance. When we are free to express the reality of what we are, we share non-personal Being.

O

125 When pure mind is manifested in the duality of the world its movement and actions are not based on personal gain, but transpersonal Being.

O

126 The habitual mind is an *addictive state* sustained by the notion of separation. So to get *'clean'* take the appropriate steps any addict must. Firstly, accept your present state is not the ultimate way you would like to live – and that something better is possible.

O

127 Secondly, contemplate whether the 'I' you see yourself to be is contented and at peace. Do you feel whole? The ego is *never* satisfied and *always* seeking to become whole. If you truly feel contented, and are at peace, then that's great. Unfortunately for most people, contentedness and peace of mind appear unobtainable because of the manner in which the mind is used. Once you establish there is a problem sustaining peace and contentment, then you can begin to deal with your addiction.

O

128   The third step in overcoming your addiction to the self is
      what you might call *mindful confrontation*. This means
      facing up to past experiences or feelings stored in your
      habitual mind. Negative memories such as notions of
      guilt, failed relationships, lingering hurt, accidents and
      illness, personal regrets, lost loved ones, ideas and
      concepts of shame all need to be recollected so that you
      can accept them. Acceptance (rather than denial) leads to
      self-forgiveness (rather than lingering guilt or blame)
      which leads to their dissolution (rather than their contin-
      uation). The reason these patterns are still there is because
      they have been hidden under the rug (so to speak) by the
      habitual mind, which means they can be recalled to your
      thoughts at any time. If they don't add to the quality of
      your life, then they are detrimental to being and should be
      let go. In order to be free, accept them, don't hide or deny
      them. Fighting these concepts only increases the sense of
      duality which allows them to linger. Likewise, continuing
      to cover or ignore these problems gives them the oppor-
      tunity to resurface. So face them and let them go. They are
      transient thoughts, emotions and memories which will
      dissolve into the nothingness from which they came.

O

129   Fear springs from the feeling of separation. Pure mind
      sees no separation and holds no fear.

O

130   Most people live within the confines of their habitual
      mind. But it is our ongoing relationship with this artificial

consciousness which continues and escalates the problem. For YOU exist perfectly well without habitual thought.

O

131   Life itself is a consequence of Sound and Light, being derived from the original explosion which created the cosmos. It is humbling to reflect that without Light and Sound, you, life and the entire Universe would not exist.

O

132   Light recognises light. If you empty your mind of habitual conditioning, you will provide the space within your consciousness to see and experience the reality of life. In this way you will simultaneously recognise, attract and encourage the same truthful and courageous qualities of Being in other forms of life.

O

133   Naked Being is the most un-mathematical reality. It gives, yet in the act of giving, it simultaneously grows, defying logic. For how can you give something and at the same time increase in it? Only because you are not giving a quantifiable measurement of some *thing*, but sharing *what* you are with *who* you are – and *that* is intelligent love.

O

134   YOU are intelligent love. There is no need to try to be this love, for YOU are already it. What stops that natural loving intelligence from being present in your life is your continued acceptance of the patterned thoughts, images

and emotions of the habitual mind. So let it all go and let your Self be free.

O

135   The ego is underrated. It provides the necessary momentum to seek and uncover your essential non-dual nature. It is your worst enemy – and yet your greatest friend.

O

136   By learning to recognise the arrival and departure of your thoughts, you gradually realise a growing sense of space in your consciousness. You are depriving the ego of the energy it requires in order to dominate your consciousness. It is being made redundant and rendered powerless. Not killed or destroyed, but dissolving through the growing recognition of what YOU are.

O

137   By learning to accept your thoughts without self-criticism, you begin to accept yourself. Don't try to stop these thoughts, just recognise the repetitive pattern of them arriving and then leaving. In doing so, their ability to dominate the way you think will be weakened. They will be recognised as cyclical and impermanent. As they continue, you become increasingly less dependent on them. With this weakening attachment to thought, the need to be judgemental begins to fade. Self-criticism, as well as the tendency to criticise or blame others, starts to fall away.

O

138   If any thought other than the present moment arises, then recognise it for what it is. Don't try to stop it but allow it to be – for in doing this you will increasingly realise the space to see beyond it. When you both allow and study the thought, it will disappear. What is real always *is*. What is unreal passes away.

O

139   By witnessing your thoughts, you are able to weed the garden of the mind. Then you begin to recognise and control the arising of thought itself. Remove the weeds to nourish each seedling that has potential. For as you know, there is little point spending time and energy fertilizing weeds when you want to grow flowers. Use the mind to transform little seeds of hope into beautiful sunflowers. You are the gardener of your own mind.

O

140   What you discover when you spend time not thinking, is that you have access to an infinite intelligent awareness which your habitual mind is only a pale reflection of. For this non-thinking pure mind is the same being-ness that is the ever-present intelligence behind stars, planets, solar systems and *all* forms of life. It is found within and outside of *all* things. Unlike a rock, a plant or a dog, you have the opportunity to recognise and realise *that* very truth within *this* very moment.

O

141   You are what you think yourself to be. And yet if you do not think, you still exist. By not thinking (while remaining completely aware) you enter the universal reality of pure mind. A process through which matter awakens to the essential truth of its founding nature.

O

142   All things which belong to you continue to be *yours* until they exist no more and then are of no further use. These things (including your body) are all useful and sometimes necessary but they can never *be* YOU. This is apparent in the way we describe things as if they are personal effects. *My* hair, *my* eyes, *my* body. Although your awareness of what is you will alter, what YOU are never changes because it is not a belonging but the permanent truth.

O

143   You say 'my body' and 'my mind' as if they are things belonging to you, so what YOU are must be the owner or user of those belongings, and not the belongings themselves. What YOU are is not the body or the habitual mind, but something existing within and beyond them both. The source of 'my' is beyond the 'I'.

O

144   The essence of what YOU are is never yours alone. There is only ONE essence. The essence of a cat, the essence of rain, the essence of a field of barley gently swaying in the breeze – all share the ONE essence.

O

145   All people are physically different, but everyone has the same vital force flowing through them. Connect to that vibrant energy in your body. Sense the life under and within every atom of your being. When you are sure you can feel this inner aliveness, take a look outside of yourself. Is it outside of you as well, in others, in the tree, or in the space directly in front of you? Where is it? Where's it not?

O

146   When we are ready to 'grow up' we will throw away the idea of separate ego-selves and accept Naked Being. For when the allure and excitement of difference fades, the original miracle of the ONE LIFE appears.

O

147   Don't think or try to become – just BE who YOU are.

O

148   Pure mind is present *before* the process of thought begins – before you begin to think, before you open your mouth, before you speak. That's why YOU are found within each and every moment.

O

149   The projections of the habitual mind obstruct reality. Pure mind on the other hand is not an experience you have, but the present *as it is* without reference to words, concepts or images. It is pure, undivided awareness in which the mind is lucid, transparent and liberated.

O

150   Naked Being is pure mind experiencing itself.

O

151   Watch your mind, but don't think about it.

O

152   When the habitual mind acquires or recognises all the forms, pleasures and sensations of the physical-emotional-material world, you still remain incomplete. You see that you have somehow fooled yourself into believing that peace and satisfaction could be found in material possessions, other people's perceptions of you, and even relationships. When this realisation dawns, you begin searching in a different way – a way that looks for the truth deep inside. Rather than continuing with the idea of evolution, you enter a spiral of involution as you begin to seek within. No longer running after further varieties of ever-changing ever-depreciating form, but looking for something that can provide permanent peace and lasting wholeness. Real peace is found by stripping back the accumulated layers of your mind to remember that YOU *are* that peace you seek.

O

153   Only that which outlasts time is of true value. Ask yourself what that timeless commodity is, and there you will find the best investment you could ever wish to make.

O

154   Growth is twofold. It manifests outwardly as the evolution of form and inwardly as the recognition of essence or Self-knowledge. Humanity is at a point of being able to integrate these two into a practical global consciousness.

O

155   Understand what you are before you attempt to grasp what you want to become. What you may become is that which YOU always are – for there is nothing else for you to become.

O

156   When you walk hand in hand with the Mind of the universe, you share that same consciousness. After all, one drop of water is as wet as an entire ocean.

O

157   Watch how the budding sunflower humbly and patiently follows the path of the sun across the sky, surrendering to the universe – sharing a profound wisdom for us all to emulate.

O

158   Within Naked Being, problems no longer control or impact your life in the same way as they used to. They are recognised as passing occurrences and not lasting personal obstructions. As sure as day follows night, they come and they go. When we recognise this cycle to be present in *all* appearances and *all* occurrences, then we find ourselves no longer attached to them but understand

that their arrival only signifies their approaching departure.

O

159 The pain felt from a headache or the pleasure of buying the house of your dreams are transient feelings which cannot last. What never arose (and so can never leave you) is the love and peace of Naked Being. It is what you were, are, and will always be. For YOU are here, now and forever.

O

160 For Naked Being never arrived and will never leave. Repeated glimpses reveal it to be permanently present, providing the knowingness you can never be separated from your essence.

O

161 Within the Heart of Naked Being there is no desire or need for you to identify with *any* personal experience, for only the ego seeks to measure and compare what *you* are and what *you* are experiencing. All objects, including the 'I' you once believed yourself to be, merge into the fullness of the present moment – so that all that is seen is THIS – the one indivisible THIS.

O

162 All form is an expression of the varying shades and differing luminosities of consciousness. The closer we are to recognising our source, the greater capability we have

to understand our True Nature. What we understand as our inherent 'divinity' is 'seen' if the mind is still, transparent and lucid. It is not some mystical secret or hidden doctrine but the way of the universe.

O

163 Awareness of Naked Being is the recognition of cosmic consciousness, realised through experiencing Universal Mind beyond the self. It is the natural path of evolution which never evolves. The home that always beckons. That pure consciousness, that YOU are in this very moment, is the same Universal Mind that Buddha and Jesus shared with the world.

O

164 In the depths of pure mind problems are easily answered and solved. Solutions are no longer sought by delving into the preferences of the habitual mind, but naturally arise from the choice-less awareness of Naked Being.

O

165 Your life will be lived according to what you believe life to be.

O

166 Suffering can only continue to occur when the ups and downs of life are experienced through the habitual mind. Likewise, peace of mind is only found in the realisation of Naked Being. It is called peace of mind because the mind has ceased all outward expectation, settling into the

tranquil consciousness YOU are.

O

167   Pure mind is like the river which flows into the sea, it doesn't decide where to go, but nevertheless arrives there effortlessly.

O

168   The word 'Heart' refers to the formless core of your innermost being. Invisible and untouchable, it points to the naked singularity – the One Heart of the One Life.

O

169   Who or what is it which listens and sees? Your answer to this question reveals your present awareness. In experiencing pure mind you do nothing – but at the same time *everything* is seen, felt and heard as the ordinary miracle of life appears.

O

170   Karma is a collection of past, present and future projections of the habitual mind. Once the habitual mind is redundant, then so is karma.

O

171   Karma does not have to come from previous lives, in fact it does not have to exist at all. YOU cannot be anything else other than pure.

O

172　Look back not only through *your* life, but through the lives of all your ancestors. Let go not only of *your* obstructions, but theirs as well. Forgive yourself – and the failings of *all* humanity.

O

173　Reincarnation is the re-formation of consciousness into individual being.

O

174　The concept of karma is a time based notion. The True Self is timeless and unchangeable. What does this mean? That both karma and reincarnation are only relative to the ego. Pure mind cannot return because it never leaves – it cannot go because there is nowhere 'else' to go to. It is the ever-present Truth.

O

175　Reincarnation is a concept arising from identification with the body combined with the mental concept of time and space. It is through sustained identification with the ego that a return to form is sought. If there is no addiction to a personal self, then there is no seeking of identification in either thought or form – just complete acceptance of Being. When you have made your way home, you will see that there is no need to take the journey again. For in truth, YOU *are* the journey and YOU *are* the home.

O

176　To experience your True Self right now, all you have to do is stop. Stop thinking, stop remembering, stop imagining and be absolutely aware of the still timeless peace YOU are.

O

177　The ego is excellent at disguise, for it exists by camouflaging your True Nature. Like an animal desperate to survive it reappears in increasingly cunning and beguiling ways.

O

178　When the obvious outer layers of the ego have been removed, the subtle sub-conscious layers begin to surface. But when what you think, say and do is attuned to the peace and intelligent love of Naked Being, the self-centredness of the habitual mind dissolves.

O

179　Rather than seeing pure mind as something to attain, remain in the timeless no-subject no-object space of Now where YOU are, for that is the truth of it.

O

180　Through conscious daily living in Naked Being, you find yourself in good health, happy and contented. This is because habitual mind-body conditioning no longer dominates your consciousness – and so you are at peace. This is the liberated order of things, the way *all* people naturally find themselves to be once the habitual mind has been withdrawn. This way of being helps others, *all* others, without seeking attention or praise and without restriction or distinction. For inherent in Naked Being is the capacity to end the suffering of the habitual mind.

O

181 Experiencing pure consciousness exposes the ego-self for what it is – a selfish, distorted way of being. By imagining reality to be self-centred, the ego obstructs the permanent peace and contentedness YOU are.

O

182 So how connected are you to pure mind? Firstly, ask yourself who is it that wants to know the answer? Secondly, as a point of reference, observe how much separation remains in your consciousness. How much of your present sense of existence is dominated by the wants, needs and thoughts of the ego-self? Giving time, space and attention to others allows the reality of what YOU are to rise to the surface of consciousness.

O

183 You cannot escape pure mind, for it is what YOU are – so your present understanding exists somewhere between ignorance and full awareness. Ignorance thrives through the ego. Awareness manifests as peace and intelligent love.

O

184 Naked Being is not something you can buy or trade. You may discover a reflection of it in another person or form, but experiencing Naked Being comes from within. Once

recognised, it is then seen to be outside of you in equal measure. As if you are a beautiful sunflower in an endless field of sunflowers all naturally following the movement of the sun. Now there is nothing to be seen but sunflowers. There is nothing to be doing but being. You are attuned to your True Nature and at one with the light of the sun.

O

185   The purpose of Naked Being is not personal gain, for your sense of ego dissolves into the reality of your True Nature. Naked Being manifests as a natural outward movement of compassion and protection for *all* living things. It is the acceptance of your natural place in the cosmic field of intelligence – the coming home to the realisation of what it means to be a human *Being*.

O

186   Looking deeper a shocking version of reality dawns – the realisation that within Naked Being there is no 'I'. The 'I' is discovered to be a habitual proposition of the ego-self. In reality there is no 'I' at the Heart of what you are, just the experiencing of indivisible pure mind. So ask yourself, who is it that needs that sense of 'I'? What would you lose from no longer identifying with the 'I'? And is it possible to be you without it?

O

187   Naked Being is the realisation of emptiness, which allows the formless nature of reality to be 'seen'. Once this 'seeing' has occurred, old values, personal beliefs and

opinions fall away as the body and habitual mind are recognised to be 'garments' of Being.

O

188 Eventually a point arises where there is no more me or 'I', for all conscious addictive thought has ceased to occupy the mind. Your consciousness becomes empty of identity, labels, emotions, thoughts and images but full of luminous space. Full of nothing. This is pure mind, the timeless unchanging reality behind the misleading overcoat of ego. It is not what *you* are, but what *all* is.

O

189 You may or may not consider yourself an Atheist, Jew, Muslim, Christian, Buddhist or a follower of any number of world religions. The reality is that YOU are none of these, yet found within all of them.

O

190 Call your belief system whatever you like, but the need to belong to any group which denies the relative truth of another, or one that believes it has *the* answers, only further contributes to the self-mistaken idea of bias and separation.

O

191 Specific teachings, beliefs and belief systems can also become attachments. If you are an X-ian or a Y-ist, your understanding and experiencing is more than likely confined to the methods and teachings of X or Y. It doesn't

guarantee *anything* apart from the inevitable division that exists between those who share your beliefs and those who do not. There is a perennial truth underlying *all* beliefs, philosophies and religions – YOU.

O

192   The freedom of Naked Being is realised when you are liberated from *all* codes and concepts, thereby transcending belief. It is within *all* people and not limited to a certain way, path or school of thought. There are more ways to realising YOU than there are stars in outer space.

O

193   To have no connection with God or pure consciousness is a common mistake – as well as an absolute impossibility.

O

194   Go beyond *any* world religion and you will find the Naked Being-ness of *all* humanity. Your True Universal Nature is beyond belief, *and that is exactly where it is found.*

O

195   To know God – stop believing in the *idea* of one.

O

196   Naked Being is not something to believe in, but Self-knowledge which has risen to the surface of consciousness. Why does this come about? Because your Nature is to establish heaven on earth.

O

197   'God is within you – as you are within God' is a long forgotten truism which has been hidden by the dust of neglect, silently waiting to be spring cleaned and brought back to life. As the thirteenth century German mystic Meister Eckhart explained it, 'God is at home, it is we who have gone out for a walk.'

O

198   Only when you have let go of all the many names and faces of God are you free. Then you realise the essence of all being is God, for *God is Being*.

O

199   The unconditional Godless God of *all* people is the ONE essence of everything that is and is not, the faceless, formless absolute reality behind and within the totality of existence, and whether this is called Lord, Allah, Yahweh, Father, Spirit, Being or Truth, the name remains unimportant. For how can you name the nameless? There are no words to describe the indescribable. Attempting to explain the reality of God is like trying to express the beauty, joy and plenitude of silence without opening your mouth.

O

200   There are two further concepts to consider regarding the existence of the divine. One is that the human being *is* God, and secondly, that there is no God. Both of which may be answered on a clear still night by looking up at the

sky. If the human being is God in totality, then he must firstly be able to recreate the universe, but can we? No! We can't even look after the tiny chunk of rock called earth that we live on! Secondly, if there is no God, no fundamental Truth behind life and existence, then we must assume that the apparent order, organisation, beauty and intelligence which are evident to our eyes in the night sky must have come about through sheer chance. If we contemplate what has the ability to create and sustain such a diverse masterpiece, we must admit from a human perspective, it appears to be the work of genius, and therefore the manifestation of mind. Not mind as we know it, but an ever-present Universal Mind beyond the reach of intellect.

O

201   Some like to enquire about God. If you asked 'What is God?' the reply would be 'What is God not?' If you asked 'Where is God?' the reply would be 'Where is God not?' If you asked 'Who is God?' the reply would be 'Who is God not?' If you asked 'Is God true?' the reply would be 'God *is* Truth'.

O

202   God cannot be confined. You can shelter from the midday sun, but there is no way of turning off the heat. Likewise, the 'Father' revered by Jesus is the 'Allah' venerated by Mohammed.

O

203   God is the ONE primordial MIND LIFE BEING TRUTH

revealed when mind and consciousness are layed bare. You are an atom in the 'body' of God, an atom that has the wonderful opportunity to consciously recognise the 'body'.

O

204   There is an exercise you can use with the name Allah or AL-LAH, for this is the sound of the breath, the source of your continuing physical existence. The first part 'AL' is the inhalation and the second part 'LAH' is your exhalation. Try it with your mouth slightly open and see. Now imagine that the life force is drawn into your body on the inhalation 'AL' and you become vitalised by this. Then the outward breath 'LAH' is the result of your intimate exchange with the universe. Try it for just a minute and see. It's a powerful tool for stilling the mind and provides insight into how the unmanifest becomes manifest. When you were born, as you gulped air into your lungs, the in breath of 'AL' was the first sound you made. When you leave this earthly existence, the exhalation of 'LAH' will be the last sound you make.

O

205   If we continually seek to find truth in the form of another we will *never* find it in ourselves. But if we look inside, then realise the inside to be a mirror of the outside, Truth is seen everywhere.

O

206   Nothing is true, yet Truth *is*.

O

207   Truth requires no conditioning, no practice, no reminder, no memorising of what it is. It doesn't need anything or anyone in order to be. It is Truth and when you recognise it, you will not need to follow a particular practice, to be constantly reminded or to continually memorise it. You will know it to be what YOU are.

O

208   'All the religions of the world, while they may differ in other respects, unitedly proclaim that nothing lives in this world but Truth.' Mohandas Gandhi (1869-1948 CE). No one can BE without Truth. Truth is beyond the limits of the senses, yet infinitely reachable.

O

209   Pure mind awareness is most transparently described as 'THIS' because that is the clearest depiction of consciousness before it becomes entangled with conditions and patterns. There is no doubt you can know THIS – for it is who YOU are.

O

210   The Self of Naked Being is neither a thought nor a form. It is the original, present and future Truth of what YOU are. That is why it is often referred to as the True Self.

O

211   Let go of any dependency on the erratic comings and

goings of the mind and the True Self will be seen to be the only permanent resident.

O

212   All perceptions of life (while appearing absolute to the senses) are edited versions of reality 'seen' in accordance with the patterning of your mind.

O

213   Realisation arises from the Self-knowledge of Naked Being. Seeing that 'I' is not YOU, but that the Self is really inherent existence. Recognising that underneath all outer appearances YOU are pure consciousness. This journey is initiated through self-effort, as the self prepares, seeks, sees, understands and then establishes realisation of the True Self. On the other hand, when the Self is realised, it requires no thought, no self-effort whatsoever. It is undeniably known to be the essence of *all*.

O

214   Awakening to Self doesn't happen to the habitual mind. It can't. Only when the habitual mind is disengaged or falls away does the ever-present Self 'appear'.

O

215   There is never a moment when the Self is not present. YOU are always here, as Truth is always here. Only when your habitual mind gets in the way does the illusion of absence appear.

O

216   You may think that Naked Being is not the Heart of what you are. But how do you know that? Who or what is it that proposes that very thought? If you believe it is *not* what you are, then you must recognise what it *is*. You know what it is because it is your underlying nature. You know what it is *not* because it is what YOU always are.

O

217   In truly letting go of the concept of a separate identity, pure mind surfaces. You no longer identify yourself as being 'I' because the ego of the habitual mind has merged into the inseparable ocean of Naked Being. The pure mind reality of YOU can never be denied. It is doubtless knowing (or knowingness) and not a theory, proposal or concept which can be considered and debated.

O

218   The intrinsic nature of what YOU are does not depend on one person. People are many, but essence is only ONE.

O

219   Naked Being goes beyond the transience of altered states and peak experiences, awakening to a sacred stillness. Your actions become naturally sensitised and no longer dependent on old patterns of 'conditioned logic'. You have simply managed to peel back the layers overshadowing Truth. It's not *your* truth, but Truth itself. You realise it to be so because you no longer have the need to identify with it – but see that everyone has unlimited

access to that same Truth.

O

220   Nothing is yours. It never was. After all what do you need to have? All you need, you already have – because all you truly have, YOU already are.

O

221   No longer lost in the recapturing of higher states of consciousness, you recognize that heaven is always here, and so is hell; they are conditional upon your awareness. Quieting the ego and the babbling brook of the habitual mind allow you to participate in the Joy of Being.

O

222   There is no 'decision' to be made about how to set about doing something, just insight leading to the answer. No longer depending on your restrictive store of logic and the snowballing of emotion, you go beyond compulsion, to reveal permanent solutions. Problems can no longer linger, because they are known to be impermanent and are dealt with as simply as sweeping the floor. There is no interference, no obstruction, no doubt, if you are following your True Nature.

O

223   Previous aspirations, desires and hopes which once directed your life are recognized for what they are. This is done by tracing the route of their coming into being. Through understanding the reasons behind any past

thought, word or deed – you reveal the source of their creation – physical, emotional, mental or Truth.

O

224   When there is no 'I' present, unmodified consciousness appears like the full colours of the rainbow. The idea of seeing and projecting yourself as a separate form has taken a subordinate role, withdrawn, controlled and no longer arising. Like a human prism, the colours of the rainbow flow through the window of your soul naturally, undisturbed, unmolested, without needing to be tampered with or altered. It is as it is. Naked Being is a clear channel of light spontaneously awakening – the full light of consciousness is apparent because no part is blocked or altered by patterns of thought or conditioning of the mind.

O

225   There are many types of existence all walking the universal life path of duality to oneness. Moving from part to whole. These millions upon millions of diverse expressions, faces and degrees all emanate from the ONE essence. The reality of that essence is consciously realised through the transparency of pure mind.

O

226   Self-realisation means awakening to the ordinary reality of the True Self. Seeing beyond habitual patterns, you reveal the knowingness that all is ONE.

O

227 Seeking, wanting, hoping and remembering, the habitual mind nervously and aimlessly wanders backwards and forwards in time. Pure mind is the ever-present here and now – the only place YOU are ever to be found. That's why the expression *'presence'* refers to the present moment awareness of pure mind.

O

228 There is no further desire to seek comfort in form. Of course you live within a form (the body) yourself, but you are more than that. You have an intellect, but you are more still. Let go of your identification with form. Let go of your accumulated dependency on intellect, memories and emotions. Then, and only then, will you unveil the free limitless Naked Being that YOU are.

O

229 When pure mind is free to act and speak, the process of conceptual thought is no longer required. To reflect on the fact that you used to believe that life required you to think when all the time, all you needed to be was YOU. Where did those old thoughts come from anyhow? They were not from YOU, but were a muddled memorised collection of concepts and emotions accumulated within the habitual mind. For the True Self cannot be anything other than unbound and free. It cannot be held or confined for it is unable to be restricted by anyone or anything. When you realise that you don't need to constantly think in order to be you, then there is tremendous peace.

O

230   When there is tremendous peace, you discover the power and beauty of silence. A silence which exists because there is no thought required and nothing else needing to be thought of. Within that blissful stillness, the oneness of existence becomes peacefully apparent and everything is realised to be perfect and whole as it is. Should you be required to act or react, you do so from the pure mind awareness of Naked Being, and not from the unawareness of the habitual mind.

O

231   The truth is that you don't need to think in order to realise the ever-present peace and harmony within. You could say that habitual thought was responsible for stopping peace and joy from being consciously present. It is ironic to see that what held you back, what stopped you from moving was the arrival of the thought that there was any moving to do. There was neither any movement to accomplish nor any decision needing to be made as to where to move in order to find the authenticity of what YOU are. For the 'movement' of the True Self takes choice-less care of itself without the need for conceptualised thought.

O

232   All forms are thoughts. All thoughts are forms.

O

233   So what is the point of the mind you ask? The point of the existence of the mind is to awaken to your True Nature, the Self. For this is the real 'purpose' of human life, to realise the unchanging spontaneous experience of Naked

Being and to actualise the pure minded-ness YOU are.

O

234   The story of the evolution of form is incredible, but the fact that a human being can recognize their formless nature or Spirit – *that* is the real miracle of life.

O

235   Everybody is looking for something because all people are in the process of finding their essence. You discover the nature of essence when you are no longer confined or limited by what you know, for then you are freed from the restrictions of fragmented ideas and limited views. Not until all acquired knowledge, concepts and under-standings are taken for what they are (and consequently let go) do you become free to 'see' the original reality YOU are.

O

236   As acquired knowledge gives way to Truth, the mind is returning to its original potential.

O

237   The intellect challenges the validity of pure mind because although it can grasp and understand ideas about the True Self, it is unable to be present in the experiencing of it. Your intellect can never prove for certain that the True Self exists, because YOU are not an 'idea' or experience which can be argued into or out of existence. YOU are the Truth of LIFE and require living in order to be known.

O

238   The 'I' which outwardly compares people overlooks the
        inner reality of YOU. Comparison with another person
        or group only provokes a sense of difference, when
        essentially, none exists. For what need is there to compare
        with another when underneath all is ONE? What is the
        comparer seeking to achieve? And why?

O

239   The True Self is often recognised through a sequence of
        encounters with the unified nature of reality, which
        eventually lead to a grounded acceptance of both who
        and what YOU are.

O

240   Ideas feed the intellect but YOU are something which
        goes beyond habitual logic and fragmentary thought. In
        Naked Being there is no requirement for the intellect to
        arise. Pure mind awareness transcends conditioned
        thought.

O

241   No matter how developed your intellect, it cannot be
        present in experiencing pure mind. Intellect thrives on the
        comparison of self or group achievement which originates
        from the desire of the ego-self. Until you give up
        attachment *to* or identification *with* your intellect, the
        difficulties of life will continue to cause you suffering. The
        intellect perceives life as a sequence of logical complex-
        ities and constantly attempts to analyse all thoughts, ideas

and outcomes as either being right or wrong according to a personal or group viewpoint.

O

242 Reason is distinguishable from intellect. Intellect acts upon stored information, memories and concepts, whereas reason deals with the present as it arises. Intellect cannot explain what is has no knowledge of, but reason may adapt to *any* experience. There is so much that the 'I' doesn't and cannot know, and yet nothing YOU need to know.

O

243 What is divided promotes division, while the inseparable encourages unification. The divisive nature of intellect reveals its real source – the ego. Substantiating the validity, power or weight of your intellect very often relies on comparing other intellects as either similar, lesser or greater. In proving itself, it seeks to expose the inferiority or superiority of another or to empower itself through identification with a specific group or level, which only continues the idea of separation. It is a disguise, a covering, one of the garbs of being, and not the naked Truth of what YOU are.

O

244 Of course some people appear 'brighter' than others, but the point being made here is not to identify what you are with the intellect. What YOU are is what *all others are*, so it cannot be the distinctive nature of intellect. Dropping all forms of distinction reveals the

ONE TRUE ESSENCE of LIFE.

O

245 Self-knowledge arises from the realisation that YOU are transpersonal essence.

O

246 Seeking begins with you and ends with YOU. The problem is the self and the solution the Self. Self-enquiry is the most direct and efficient way of establishing your True Nature because it goes directly to the cause (you) to establish the cure (YOU).

O

247 Reality is seen once the charade of the ego gives way, for only then are you no longer thinking, projecting or imagining. When your habitual identity steps out of the way, no further obstructions to Naked Being remain.

O

248 Your ability to think is not what YOU are, because it has the capacity to change and develop. It is knowledge acquired by the self and for the self, projected through the habitual mind. On the other hand, Self-knowledge is unchanging and unchangeable. It cannot grow or develop because it has always existed *outside* of ego, time and space and is not subject to change. So your intellect cannot presently be or have ever been what YOU are. Without your intellect, you are not lost, on the contrary, YOU will be found by seeing it for what it is – and going beyond it.

O

249 Pure mind goes beyond the acquired knowledge of the self, appearing far too radical to be true from the viewpoint of the habitual mind. The ego simply doesn't want to accept the reality that there is something more real, more funda-mental to life than itself. If it did, it would be forced to surrender to it. That surrender would mark the end of its domination and the beginning of its demise. The intellect is only a minute, fragmented realisation of the mind's limitless potential and cannot perceive the vastness of universal intelligence without yielding to it. So step out of the way and step in to the reality of what YOU are.

O

250 Your intellect doesn't realise it is only struggling against itself. One day it will simply give up – and give in to reality.

O

251 When the Self is known, the concept of individual knowledge, intellect and intelligence are seen as veils of Being and not the Truth of LIFE. Only Self-knowledge (the Self when known as pure consciousness) is true and lasting.

O

252 Self-knowledge *is* reality.

O

253   Preconceived ideas only get in the way of Self-knowledge.
        The belief that you know more than another only proves
        the habitual mind has been engaged. To the Self, it would
        be more true to say 'I know nothing' – for the 'I' cannot
        realise the Truth of what YOU are. Accumulating nothing
        and holding no belief, Self-knowledge of BEING, is 'I-less'
        and indivisible.

O

254   The unsatisfiable ego doesn't stop with you. Because of
        what you are thinking, saying and doing here and now,
        your children and your children's children may continue
        to believe that the truth of what they are lies in their
        differences. Truth is revealed when the ONE essence is
        acknowledged to underlie *all* appearances.

O

255   The concept of death arises from bodily identification.
        The body will not and cannot last because it is only a
        temporary form of housing. Once death is seen to be just
        the shedding of a skin, the emptying of a shell, then you
        are freed from bodily identification.

O

256   Accept now that your body will one day be worn out and
        eventually cease to exist. When your habitual mind
        ceases, you realise that YOU live for ever.

O

257   To the True Self, birth and death are misconceptions. They

are phases or layers of being, only 'appearing' absolute to the habitual mind. To pure mind, birth and death are both elements of the ONE LIFE.

O

258 The fear of death only exists because of the ignorance of LIFE. That fear arises from the idea of the loss of a self. The True Self can never be lost. Death 'appears' due to the wear and tear of the physical body and ignorance of essence. All matter gradually and inevitably deteriorates. But YOU are beyond matter.

O

259 A near death experience provides you with absolute proof that you are not just your body. As you lose identification with your body and habitual mind, all your problems and fears drop away and you are left with a childlike purity and a feeling of absolute peace. There is no panic or anxiety because they can no longer arise. How pointless all that mental and emotional noise was. How beautifully peaceful this is. You become acutely conscious of existence beyond form. There is no struggle, no fight just the choice-less surrender to formlessness. In many ways it is the ultimate lesson in acceptance and something you can undertake here and now. Surrender NOW to the idea of your inevitable physical death in order to realise lasting peace.

O

260 When you are in a body, you are Naked Being; when you are no longer in a body, you are Naked Being. Whatever

occurs, YOU will always be, for when the body becomes uninhabitable, your abode changes accordingly. So if you can accept the eventual demise of your body *now*, then you will realise what remains when the shell of the body is no more.

O

261   What you are was born and will die. Who YOU are is LIFE ITSELF.

O

262   Death is not the end of YOU, just the ending of your present earthly form.

O

263   You cannot die if you were never born. What YOU are was never born and yet one day the body recognised to be you *will* pass away.

O

264   Time and anxiety, desire and jealousy, body and death, all are inseparable. Without time anxiety could not arise, without desire, jealousy would not be and without bodily identification, the absolute finality of death is impossible.

O

265   You are born Naked Being and you die Naked Being. Before and after these apparent events, you remain Naked Being. That's how infinite YOU are.

O

266 The habitual mind is always becoming and yet cannot become anything. Pure mind just *is*, for there is nothing else for it to become.

O

267 When your body ceases and is unable to be inhabited, it will be no more. YOU though, will continue to live on. Death holds no finality; it is just like growing sufficiently to enable the leaving of your mother's womb in order to enter a bright new world. Today you are here in the womb of the world of form, and when that tomorrow comes you will be in a different guise, in different surroundings, but YOU will still BE.

O

268 The soul is the travelling consciousness enabling discovery of your True Nature. This individual soul is *your* soul, something belonging to you and therefore not the non-dual Self of pure consciousness. The soul exists as a projection of duality because it 'thinks itself to be' – dying and becoming reborn. However, this soul is the much needed mechanism for merging the non-dual with the dual, in order that your essential Spirit Nature can be actualised in the world.

O

269 The human soul progresses through unconditional giving. Giving up (recognizing and letting go of your ego-self), giving in (realising your True Self) and giving out (sharing

or actualising your True Nature). This is the real opportunity presented by our human experience.

O

270   Soul evolution cannot be measured by the passing of time or through the number of years a person has apparently lived or studied. However, it may be clearly witnessed over time by what a person does or says, for these are tangible reflections of what someone truly thinks both they and reality are.

O

271   When you contemplate the body, it is seen to be *your* body, a body that belongs to you. Likewise when you contemplate the mind it appears as *your* mind and at a deeper level *your* soul. Naked Being is what YOU are, and what we all are – everything else is just a Chinese whisper of that Truth, a diluted version of reality.

O

272   Because the essence of what you are is not born, then neither can it be reborn. For how can something whole perceive a fraction of itself as being complete? The notion of separate being arises from overlooking the truth that YOU are already and always whole.

O

273   The fly born in a human house remains ignorant that his life is spent trapped within the limits of the four walls of that building. His world becomes a cyclical pattern of

desire, avoidance, stress and survival. Eventually becoming caught tight in a spider's web, he has failed to recognise the limitless space that lay waiting outside through the frequently open windows.

O

274 Truth is not what you presume it to be, it is what YOU are. Truth is not found in 'I' but in the presence and essence of YOU. Freedom is the expression of this essence.

O

275 Accepting Truth means going beyond what you hope and expect – to merge with what *IS*.

O

276 So what is love? Unconditioned, pure, natural love is the ongoing recognition of oneness. This love is YOU in action. So it is Naked Being you are sharing and experiencing when love is found beyond form.

O

277 The primordial qualities arising from Naked Being are intelligent love and peace of mind. It is intelligent because it knows what to do and how to go about it without engaging in the process of independent thought. It is peace of mind because nothing is sought, needed or required in order to be. It knows it is LIFE. In knowing itself, it knows *all* 'others'.

O

278   To follow Self – walk away from the self.

o

279   Pointing to the authentic basis of human consciousness has been traditionally represented by 'I AM'. Naked Being is not yours, not something the 'I' can have or is, but complete, pure unabridged awareness belonging to all. In this sense it is beyond the 'I'. When experiencing pure mind consciousness, it is not something you point to, for it is seen to be what everything and everybody already *IS*. If *I* am pointing and attempting to describe something it must exist outside of me and therefore is best described as THAT. If it is something that is presently within awareness, something that is living and being lived, then it is THIS – for then all that *IS* – is recognised to be inseparably residing within the present moment.

o

280   'Pure' minded-ness is not about never having done anything wrong in your life. It is about being what you are beyond the conditioning of the habitual mind, surrendering to the reality of what *IS*. For when there is no continuing resistance, no ongoing desire of 'self' 'else' or 'other', habitual consciousness has returned to its original source. Now, like a wind chime moved within the breath of an inseparable universe, any 'music' made is harmoniously in tune with the totality. The result is uncreated and created, silent and audible, for it is the unmanifest manifested.

o

281   The process of 'purification' requires the ongoing honesty
       of admitting to all your faults and seeing them for what
       they are – life lessons. To continually bare yourself *warts
       and all*, in the words of Oliver Cromwell, is a vital step
       towards the baring of your True Nature. If you continue to
       delude yourself with synthetic versions of what *you* want
       reality to be, or how *you* would prefer it to turn out, then
       you neglect your True Nature which is inseparable from
       the way reality *IS*.

O

282   Wash away your camouflage, remove your makeup and
       accept Truth. You are perfect as you originally are, as
       pristine as you could ever *now* be. YOU are the timeless
       presence, the 'AM-ness' before, within and beyond
       Abraham.

O

283   Forgiveness is part of the paradox of life. If you cannot
       forgive another, you will never be able to forgive yourself.
       If you cannot forgive yourself, you will never know how
       to forgive another.

O

284   If all is perceived by states of mind, Naked Being is best
       described as the pure minded way. This process of 'going
       beyond identity' refers to arriving at a point where the
       habitual consciousness no longer gets in the way of your
       pure minded nature. For then you become aware of what
       YOU are in the clearest, most *illogical* way.

O

285   The way forward is not to continually establish freewill, but to give in to your True Nature. For although human identity in the shape of the body and mind is perceived as separate and individual, underlying essence is not. Recognising and relinquishing the notions of the habitual mind allows a gradual dissolution of the old patterns of the ego, eventually arriving at the choice-less peace of pure mind. Stepping aside, you surrender to the unblemished consciousness of THIS.

O

286   Unresolved problems derive themselves from the habitual mind. In pure mind there are no lingering problems because they are resolved by acceptance rather than opposition. Acceptance is the key to the resolution of *any* problem. Don't fight it, but let it unfold, for in doing so it will resolve itself.

O

287   Truth requires the courage to let go of the habitual layers of projected personality, disguise, comfort, protection and security, thereby exposing the invisible peace and intelligent love of Naked Being.

O

288   Characteristics of pure mind include intrinsic awareness, compassion for LIFE and independence from acquired knowledge. Only in this way do you remain detached and yet connected, leaving you free to merge with reality.

O

289   When there is no preconceived idea about the past or future, no seeking or striving and no desired result to achieve, then you are naturally experiencing the Joy of Being. It is naturally uplifting because you are the Source of LIFE experiencing itself.

O

290   Pure consciousness is manifested through pure mind, but otherwise, like the air you breathe, it remains invisible and undetected.

O

291   Definitive ideas are obstructions. If you cannot accept an experience and at the same time leave it behind, your awareness does not remain free to grow. For if there is holding on, who is holding on, and to what are they holding on to? What YOU are cannot be let go, so there is nothing to lose.

O

292   There is such a thing as destiny, but all destinies are ONE. There is such a thing as freewill to be yourself or desire to be other than YOU are, but there is no personal will in pure mind for no individual is present to instigate the idea.

O

293   Surrendering yourself to pure mind allows you to discover

that the mystery which pervades you also pervades the entire universe. For that which is everywhere is in us – and that which is in us is everywhere.

O

294   Experiencing Naked Being is the divine experience, realised when the ego-self is silenced and still. Therefore if you know your Self you will know the meaning and reality of the divine.

O

295   All forms are, at best, poor representations of the truth. If you wish to see truth as a form, then who is it that desires to witness form? For that which is identified in form alone has a mind turned to form and so perceives form. But that which identifies with the formless has a mind turned to formlessness and sees beyond form.

O

296   Dwelling in non-duality you see there was never anything of yours to surrender, there is no 'I' or 'me' in Naked Being, your desired will is non-existent and reality itself is devoid of the presence of the beguiling ego. You desire and expect nothing, but live in the vibrant reality of the present moment.

O

297   Pure mind has no drive or ambition, yet is inherently creative for it spontaneously expands.

O

298   Pure mind has no interest in escaping cycles of birth and death for it is knowingly present in both. The very idea of wanting to escape mistakenly promotes the idea that there is something to escape *from* and somewhere else to go *to* other than the here where YOU always are. This notion is a time and space projection brought about by the habitual mind. In pure mind then there is nothing to run towards or away from. Here is only ever here, for YOU can be nowhere 'else'.

O

299   Let go of all expectation to experience Truth.

O

300   There is knowledge acquired by the self and there is Self-knowledge. Only one is lasting. Only one is Universal Wisdom.

O

301   You were born into the world when you were separated from your mother at birth. You are reborn *as the world* through knowing the Self, the ONE True Self.

O

302   Apparent gifts, like apparent misfortunes, provide a way to recognise the truth of what YOU are. They appear as separate direct personal experiences, and yet provide the same window of opportunity to realise the ONE *transper-*

sonality of the Self.

O

303　Transpersonality is the expression of the ONE unchanging nature of Being. Beyond the notion of a separate ego-self, these shared characteristics of Being manifest as *peace of mind* and *intelligent love*. When you are really in touch with your Self, you are ONE with all life, for you are LIFE.

O

304　YOU and my Self are inseparable. At a deep level of Being there is no distinction. Everything you see or experience in the world is the blossoming awareness of the ONE True Self, the consciousness of complete surrender in which no 'I' or anything 'else' *IS*. In surrendering to reality, you merge with it.

O

305　The habitual mind is the refuse storage system of human consciousness. When will you empty yourself and realise the clarity YOU are?

O

306　The search for identity arises from the ego-self. If there is no ego dominating or controlling, the need to seek or assume a separate identity subsides and your natural connection with the universe resumes.

O

307   Let everything go and *all* will come to you.

O

308   Oneness is the sole reality beyond the passing dream of form.

O

309   'Remain in your own formations, but rise above body-consciousness, rise into universalism and leap into the beyond, and know you are already one.' Sant Kirpal Singh (1894-1974 CE) – Nothing to do, nowhere to go, no one to be other than the Self. Let go of the tiny splinter you are, and the tree of LIFE will appear.

O

310   Ask yourself who is it that denies oneness? It is the same entity which obstructs you from seeing it and being it.

O

311   It is rare in life that fortune provides us with the skills of a great teacher, but the greatest by far is within you. The habitual mind provides experiences and drives the seeking of Self-knowledge which leads to the peace and pure minded wisdom of Naked Being.

O

312   Unexpected is an interesting word. For nothing is expected or unexpected if you are truly awake in the present moment. When the mind is pure and presently

aware, pictures and dramas come and go but reality remains the same as it ever is. Events come and go in a similar fashion to the rising and setting of the sun, and whether the sky appears clear blue or pitch black, it remains the sky. As you are always YOU.

O

313   Situations, events and what you interpret others do and say may result in you becoming annoyed, agitated or frustrated, but you only allow yourself to be affected in this way because of your continuing dependence on the habitual mind. These happenings are only perceived as 'against you' because they are seen from the perspective of the seemingly separate 'I' personality. But when there is no separate 'I' to be found, nothing can be contrary to YOU, as all is revealed to be the ONE True Self. Then there is no other, no separate personality left to feel annoyed, unsettled or irritated.

O

314   Pure mind is complete undivided attention and full awareness without the personal wants and desires of the ego-self.

O

315   You cannot intellectualise Truth, only concepts. Truth is non-personal, concept-less and what it is. Even the most basic statement such as 'the sky is blue' is not Truth. Only concepts can be objectively studied as being true or untrue. Truth is unarguably here. Ego debates Truth, pure mind lives it.

O

316   When the sun shines on a cloudless day we feel the full benefit of its warm rays. Clouds only obstruct the light if they are between you and the sun. For where do the clouds in your life come from and what stops you from bathing in the sunlight?

O

317   Pure mind has no hopes and dreams. It is neither imagined nor attained.

O

318   Experiencing the True Self is the same as experiencing another's because they are inseparable. The ONE True Self does not 'belong' to any one person. It may appear as an identifiable individual form on the surface but it is not really so, for Truth is not within some but all. Realisation means awakening to the ONE inherent essence of *all* people, *all* life.

O

319   The True Self and the ONE True Self are the same. This is only hard to come to terms with if you are still clinging to the notion of a separate identity. For if you are awakened to the reality of Naked Being, there is no appearance of separation just the unequivocal sense of unification. This means that although you still see the world as it was proposed by the habitual mind, the sense of it revolving around the 'I' is no longer there. The 'I' as a focal point has gone. This is oneness – experiencing all from an indivisible

pure consciousness – knowing that the True Self is indivisible essential Being. For in reality all is the ONE True Self, for *all is Being*.

O

320 Once the ONE True Self has been 'seen' it can never be denied but experiencing may come and go because there is often a transitional period when the habitual mind continues to arise as it struggles to regain influence. The time this revolution lasts is down to you, for time is only proposed by the habitual mind. But like all greedy and forceful dictators it will eventually be toppled. For the more often pure mind is felt or experienced, the deeper the realisation, and the greater the reduction of the thought patterns of the ego-self. Ironically it is the habitual mind which serves as the key to its own downfall because it is the seeking, desiring mechanism which allows the experiencing of pure mind to be initially awakened and then pursued.

O

321 There may come a time when pure mind is sought after, which indicates a return to the grasping nature of the habitual mind. If this continues without accompanying growth, then you are continuing to perceive pure mind as something quite separate from you. Perhaps it is seen as a state to attain, a place of peace you go to, or a practice you repeat in order to reach a higher state of consciousness. The truth is that these 'states' are actually brief encounters with your True Nature. They are what you experience as you increasingly surrender to reality. When these glimpses or episodes subside, then the need to see pure

consciousness as 'something' 'someone' or 'somewhere' else has fallen away. As Self-knowledge merges with pure consciousness, what was once experienced as a mystical or altered state becomes grounded and ordinarily real.

O

322   Realising the ONE True Self doesn't mean that you lose your identity, but rather that you end the concept of duality. Oneness is something you have always sensed, yet been unable to understand because it is something the logical and pre-conditioned intellect cannot grasp.

O

323   Experiencing oneness there is nothing to find, nothing to gain, for it is pointless to search for something YOU already are. In oneness, nothing apparently exists outside of the ONE LIFE and no continuing search is felt to be required for you are 'one with all things'. The habitual mind will seek to return by clinging even to this experience, but let it come and go until it passes without altering your perception.

O

324   When you see that oneness is not an altered state experience that you can have or are given – but an undivided momentary blending with the Spirit YOU are, then it cannot be ignored or forgotten. Experiencing oneness is getting to know Self.

O

325   Looking into the eyes of a realised person, you see the Self. Listening to their words, you hear the Self. A realised person is simply a mirror for Being, no more, no less. When the gazer and the reflection are known as ONE, the Truth of LIFE appears.

O

326   When you permanently identify with the notion of a hierarchy, it separates you from what YOU are. As a spiritual seeker, the presence of a hierarchy often encourages you to find yourself in the form or image of another. The days of the Prophet and Guru are no more. Undertake whatever spiritual practice or study you require in order to still and transcend the habitual mind, for that transcendence is the real purpose and goal behind all teachings and practices. The most beneficial practice you can undertake is to BE YOU as often as possible. After all, do you need to continually practice walking to be able to walk? Or continually practice breathing in order to presently breathe? There comes a point where practice is no longer required, because you are living the LIFE found *within* the practice.

O

327   The ONE True Self does not cling to anything. Not to knowledge, identity or ideas. It is through not knowing that one arrives at the realisation that you know nothing, for there is nothing you need to know in order to be YOU.

O

328   Not to seek or avoid. Not to want or to lack. Acceptance

and allowance of what is – this is the way to Wholeness and freedom.

O

329   Thinking that there was a door to go through is revealed as the greatest misleading proposition of the habitual mind. Now you are 'here', you see that 'here' is where you always were. No distinction exists between inside and outside because it is the ONE whole, so they were never separated in the first place. Any idea of difference and separation was just an illusion of the habitual mind.

O

330   The notion of suffering is a habitual mistake. The idea 'I am suffering' arises from the belief and acceptance of a separate self. Suffering will continue until you recognise that it is the *thought* of suffering which makes you unhappy, and not the experience itself. The experience came and went. Your True Nature cannot suffer because it is not affected by ideas and thoughts. Only the habitual mind can let you endure an idea.

O

331   Suffering is distinct from pain. Pain is a physical body sensation, whereas suffering is a mind condition. In a child, for example, look at what happens if they fall over in the playground. Firstly, there is an action (the leg is grazed) followed by the onset of body pain and the reactionary thought 'I have fallen over and my leg hurts'. The depth of suffering will depend on the length of time the child continues to identify with the idea of being hurt.

The leg which is grazed may well produce physical pain for a short while, but the prolongation of suffering is a self-induced condition. This is why a child who is comforted, distracted or offered a treat soon forgets about suffering. Their thoughts are elsewhere. It is only thought which allows suffering to persist. Have you ever looked into the eyes of someone who has completely accepted the inevitability of their approaching physical death? There you find the most incredible peace. A profound, sustainable peace beyond words and a truthful elegant beauty unable to be replicated. Suffering has been transcended, and they are FREE.

O

332   As time passes you feel no identity with the idea of 'me', 'I' or 'mine' and see no separation, for all aspects or notions of duality dissolve.

O

333   The concepts you had of the divine also fall away because the experiencing of oneness reveals your existence to be inseparable from *all* else. You see no division between Buddha, God, Christ, Krishna and all people, all things, all non-things.

O

334   If you remove *everything* in the way of pure mind, you will be aware of the undivided Nature of the ONE True Self. When grounded in this Nature, it is undoubtedly 'known' to be concept-less Truth. The knowingness which surfaces does not come from any sense or desire of the self, but

arrives directly and spontaneously by experiencing Naked Being.

O

335   You look for what YOU are, but YOU already know. YOU remain the essence of what you seek. YOU have nothing to get, nothing to find, for nothing is found or gained when pure mind is realised.

O

336   Distinction does not mean absolute difference, for unity is revealed through acknowledging the interconnectedness of diversity. Buddha had nothing that YOU don't have, but he was able to realise pure mind and to actualise that in the duality of the world. So what is the difference between you and Buddha? Your present state of mind, for YOU and Buddha are ONE. So to be Buddha, BE YOU – for YOU *are* Buddha.

O

337   So the seeker becomes the sought – which are both revealed to be ONE. There was no one to become and no becoming to undertake. Naked Being is true meaning beyond words. A pure spontaneous expansion of universal consciousness without attachment to identity or gain. It is yours. It is ours. It is everyone's. It is the transpersonal THIS.

O

338   When the sense of 'I' merges with the Self, then all is THIS.

O

339 *Who am I?* When you know the answer to this question, then *you* are no more, for YOU are consciously present.

O

340 YOU cannot change. If what you perceive as being YOU can change or is something which can be changed, then it is not YOU. The body will fade away in time. The habitual mind is constantly changing as concepts, ideas and beliefs continue to come and go. Only Naked Being timelessly remains.

O

341 The habitual mind camouflages the essential THIS-ness of pure mind. Pure mind disguises nothing for it is completely free to BE.

O

342 THIS is the clearest description of the consciousness of pure mind. It is unlocked beyond the primary thought of 'I AM'. Any 'I' by its very nature falls short of transpersonal Being. 'I' is only a concept. THIS is not a concept but REALITY itself. THIS is *always* present and does not require the presence of the 'I' in order to be, for it is not the 'I' that sees THIS, but THIS which sees the 'I'. THIS does not and cannot personally belong for it is unobstructed by any and all conditioning. It is the clearest description of experiencing Universal Mind. Connected with all, unbound and fully merged with the oneness of reality, consciousness ultimately recognises itself as the timeless THIS.

O

343   The distinctive thought of 'I' is only required if there are other 'I's' to be found. When no 'I' is perceived to exist at all, then 'I AM' dissolves to reveal the indivisible pure consciousness of THIS. Without identity, without needs or requirements it is the undiluted presence of stillness itself.

O

344   The 'I' causes confusion because it is a misrepresentation of what YOU are. When reality is seen, there is no 'I' to be found. As the revelation of 'I AM' fades, YOU merge with the formless reality of LIFE itself.

O

345   *This we have now*
Is not imagination.
This is not
grief or joy

Not a judging state,
or an elation
or sadness.
Those come
and go.

This is the presence
that doesn't.

This that we are now
created the body, cell by cell,
like bees building a honeycomb.

The human body and the universe
grew from this, not this
from the universe and the human body.

Jelalludin Balkhi *aka* Rumi (1207 – 1273 CE)

O

346 Realising the ONE True Self is a natural process brought about by surrendering the ego-self to pure mind.

O

347 Pure mind is effortless being beyond concepts, the present moment awareness pointed to by the expressions such as 'I AM THAT'. However, if we are unable to go beyond these words to the actual meaning and experiencing of being ONE with the I-ness, That-ness or Am-ness itself, it denotes that the mind is still separated to a degree. If it is something you are integrally part of, it cannot be described as 'that' for 'that' suggests something quite separate from you, something being pointed to – and therefore duality. In the depths of Naked Being there is no 'I', no 'I am', no 'that', only the living presence of THIS. For even the primary thought 'I AM' arises out of the pure mind transpersonal consciousness of THIS. The existence of 'I' in *any* form dissolves. For who or what is it which requires the presence of 'I'? Only an 'I' apprehensive of losing its identity in the absolute needs to retain the notion of an 'I'. Does pure consciousness *need* an 'I'? Being one and all, it requires no primary thought and no identity. It is simply THIS.

O

348   There is nothing outside of THIS, for it is the silent awakening of the present moment, the complete conscious recognition of the Now. When presently aware of the pure consciousness YOU are, then THIS is the clearest description of that unified reality.

O

349   So to point to the presence of Naked Being most clearly is to suggest the experiencing as THIS, letting go of your safely guarded separate identity to see that at the deepest level all life is interconnected, transpersonal and inseparable. THIS is indivisible whereas the use of either 'that' or 'I' suggest otherwise. This is because the very idea of 'I' remains central to the notion of individual identity, which in turn provides an open window through which the separateness of the ego-self may resurface. By identifying with 'I', the tendency is for the ego-self to grasp at the opportunity to reinstate itself, seeking to reconstruct a mental world of conceptual barriers and separate identities. At the end of the day any perception of 'I' is only a name, a thought and a proposition. Let go of all names, thoughts and forms and you will awaken THIS.

O

350   Your apparent identity remains unchanged – but you know that as a human being, you are pure consciousness manifested through a mind, residing within a body. You are still a mother, a brother, a daughter, a son. What you are remains unchanged for you can only let go of what you never were. As a crystal is Spirit in the form of a mineral, or a flower is Spirit in the form of a plant, you are

Spirit in the form of a human. All is Being.

O

351   Now you are living life *as it is*. You are not getting in the way with personal wants, needs and desires. You understand it would be pointless to do so. There is nothing to worry about, nothing in the way, just THIS, simply THIS, only THIS.

O

352   The realisation of pure mind is enough. Accept it and don't complicate it – for it is not something complex. Complication leads you back into the habitual mind. For clarity, like Truth, is simple.

O

353   Emptiness. Don't be confused by the word. Emptiness refers to the illusory nature of all phenomena. When you are empty, YOU are seen to fill all space.

O

354   Ideas about Truth can always be intellectually challenged. However, Truth itself cannot be disputed by anyone, for who is present to challenge it? When you realise Truth, then you have merged with the anonymous reality.

O

355   Mind need not be confined to the brain or permanently attached to the idea of individual being. Once you peel

back and uncover the unmodified reality of pure mind, consciousness is realised to be free, boundless and all pervading.

O

356 Of course you have parents, but YOU were never born. Attachments to family are often the hardest to overcome. They may contain unresolved issues of comparison, favour and lack of love and support that need to be dealt with. The family you have is for very good reason – to help you learn and grow. This learning continues until you realise that at the deepest level of Being, LIFE is your family. We can find a reflection of this in the New Testament of the Bible. 'There came then his brethren and his mother, and, standing without, sent unto him, calling him. And the multitude sat about him, and they said unto him, Behold, thy mother and thy brethren without seek for thee. And he answered them, saying, Who is my mother, or my brethren? And he looked round about on them which sat about him, and said, Behold my mother and my brethren!' (Mark 3:31-34). A deeper understanding of our 'spiritual' parentage can be uncovered from contemplating John 10:30 where Jesus exclaims: 'I and the Father are one' – for this seemingly egotistical yet ultimately true statement echoes a profound saying in the ancient Hindu scripture the Mandukya Upanishad. The phrase 'Ayam Atma Brahma' translates as 'This individual Self is one and the same with the absolute reality'. What does all this point to? That identification of the Self with the Absolute is the uncontaminated awareness that the Truth of Life is ONE, for in Truth there is only ONE LIFE.

O

357 YOU remain changeless and the same, permanent and always.

O

358 Living in accordance with your True Nature (being YOU) means not trying to be 'somebody' or to attain 'something' but to remain exactly 'where' YOU are. Staying grounded in the Self reveals the Truth of LIFE.

O

359 If you seek confirmation from others that you have realised the Truth of what you are, then you have not. For we know the seeker, it is the hoper and the doubter. If you think yourself to be the only one or something more than others, then consciousness is not grounded in pure mind – and you are experiencing a transient or distorted version of it. The ego cunningly and repeatedly tries to interfere and obstruct YOU, until eventually it can't. Then the mind remains pure and transparent, yet firm and doubtless. In the end no proof is required. *Presence establishes Truth.* For who can confirm what you are? Only YOU – and YOU have no need or desire to confirm *anything.*

O

360 Truth is about being ordinary rather than special. YOU are not special. To be special implies comparison for the sake of establishing distinction. In Naked Being there is no distinguishable 'other' to compare with, for everyone and everything is understood to be a unique expression of the same ONE LIFE. So who is it that dwells on the notion of special-ness in themselves and others? Only someone

incomplete and divided from their True Nature. Special-ness is the dream food of the ego. The cream tea of the habitual mind. In Naked Being, nobody and nothing is special, for special-ness is realised to be a subtle way of encouraging division and prolonging segregation.

O

361   To be 'born again' or 'awakened' is an individual experience of pure mind, whereas Self-realisation is the permanent unthought non-belief that pure consciousness is *everyone's* True Nature.

O

362   The proposition of opposites is only relative to awareness. Take the difference between day and night for example. They appear quite different – but night only exists because of day – and day only exists because of night. Day is night with sunlight. Night is day without sunlight. Both together make up the 24 hours of what is seen to be the cycle of a complete day. Each exists *only* because of the relative existence of each other. The day begins with the arrival of the sun and ends with its departure. The night begins when the sun goes down and is only complete with its rising. So both day and night are not separate, but realised according to the movement of the sun. Like your habitual and pure mind, they can be seen to be mutually dependent realities contributing to a greater whole.

O

363   Not accepting, not rejecting. No extremes. Acceptance of what *IS*. This is the Way. To only want Truth, Self, Reality

is the secret to lasting peace and contentedness. Being what YOU are and what *IS*, it is effortless unobstructed BEING.

O

364   Lasting awareness of who YOU are takes place when both attachment to 'you' and detachment from 'you' no longer arise.

O

365   Spontaneous and selfless, present in all forms and formless varieties of life, THIS is the undying consciousness of the never born.

O

366   When the seeker and the sought are revealed to be ONE, and no identity is found within, then what is left is THIS. No needs, no wants, no fears, no doubts, no desires, nothing to be known or unknown, just what is here and now. There is nothing more to strip away. After all the ups and downs, all the seeking – THIS is what is found. THIS is what, who, why and where YOU always were.

O

367   Nothing is driven. No one remains to be driven. No 'I', no me, no other, no separation. Life arises from the flow of the universe and not from the desires of ego.

O

368   With no dependency or reliance, there is no addiction. With no ongoing addiction or clinging to identity, there is no continued obstruction. 'Clean' from any habits and free from *all* obstructions, unmodified pure mind is liberated Being.

O

369   Words are useful ways of pointing to THIS – but ultimately they are not it. They cannot be. At best, words may be recognised as being moved by the wind of Truth. They are words, simply words, and not Truth itself. For the Truth of Life is only found within you, and not in any words.

O

370   THIS is your awakened inner nature experiencing itself.

O

371   Enlightenment is the knowingness that un-enlightenment has no foundation in Being. (At the Heart of human beingness everyone is already enlightened awareness.)

O

372   Enlightenment has many faces but only ONE Nature – *YOURS*.

O

373   For when everything seen and unseen is no more, when the real and unreal dissolve within each other, then all that

is left is THIS. No longer misled by appearance, label or name. Consciousness re-enters the duality of the world while retaining direct knowledge of its non-dual nature, thereby bringing about Wholeness of Being.

O

374 Beyond any ego or identity, the 'I' is revealed to be the consciousness of THIS. Without concepts, beliefs or ideas THIS belongs to no one and exists nowhere, yet remains infinitely present.

O

375 Thinking of oneself as the centre of the universe empowers the ego. Not thinking of oneself as separate from *anything* allows THIS consciousness to surface.

O

376 The invisible air we breathe has no evolution of form to undergo, for like YOU, it is already and always free.

O

377 Truth is not about what is real or unreal. The real and unreal both arise from Truth. Truth is absolutely free and whole, without needs, reliance or requirements.

O

378 Walk away from all ideas and forms of separation for then when nothing remains divided you have arrived at THIS where there is no longer distinction or difference.

O

379   You are a concept. Christ is a concept. Buddha is a concept. Enlightenment is a concept. God is a concept. Let go of all concepts, all identities – for then only THIS remains.

O

380   THIS is not a personal reality. It is transpersonal Truth.

O

381   There is no teacher and no teaching. For you cannot be taught what YOU already are. Just remove what stands in the way.

O

382   Once you surrender to pure mind you become the experiencing of pure consciousness. Not one who experiences, but at one with experiencing. THIS is Being without wants, needs or requirements.

O

383   Unable to be attached to intellect, group philosophy, belief systems, methodologies, mysteries and secrets it is always pure, always true. As YOU are always YOU.

O

384   As soon as THIS is translated through the written or spoken word, it becomes diluted. The non-dual becomes tainted by patterns and opinions. Through repeated expla-

nations it becomes increasingly modified and progressively remote from the original Truth.

O

385   For the awareness of THIS is not a form or a thought. It is unabbreviated reality without needs or requirements, with no reliance on anything or addiction to something or somebody – *it is as it is*. Pure consciousness is realised through a natural filtering of the mind to a point where consciousness becomes immersed in its naked pristine essence. So when your mind is completely unhindered, YOU are absolutely present.

O

386   Openly sharing the reality of what we all are is the only way forward for life on earth.

O

387   Be free from all you know and then you will be present within the Truth of LIFE. For when you surrender to Truth without interference – you become it.

O

388   The Buddhists believe only that which doesn't come and go is truly 'real'. Everything else is seen as 'temporary' and unable to last, and therefore said to be 'unreal'. What appears – disappears, but that which is beyond time, is, was and will always BE. In you it is the consciousness of Naked Being, the awareness of THIS, the reality YOU are.

O

389 There is no destruction of the ego-self, but a gradual purification, purging and overseeing of its host, the habitual mind. When the idea of duality no longer arises, the subject you once believed yourself to be also fades. Then there is just THIS. The pure unblemished mind contains no thoughts of separation or attachment. THIS is pure consciousness without needs, wants or desires.

O

390 Pure mind is the translator between the perceived world and Truth.

O

391 Realising the pure mind of Self is the way to freedom for *all*.

O

392 The limitations of your mind are defined by the degree to which you accept limitlessness.

O

393 As human beings it is our purpose to share what we are with each other by dualising the non-dual and habitual-ising the pure.

O

394 Found within *all* people, not restricted by race or creed,

background or belief and with no unique or absolute method of being taught, THIS spontaneously awakens through an intuitive process of inner discovery.

O

395   Attentive mind free to BE is the liberated awareness of THIS.

O

396   Form could not exist without sufficient space in which to express itself and space would not exist without the appearance of form. Likewise, mind cannot be known without consciousness and the pure consciousness YOU are cannot be known without undressing the patterning of the habitual mind.

O

397   If there is no holding on to identity, there is no illusion. When there is no illusion then no one remains to cling to the idea of identity. For when you remove the transient outer layers of being, only the transpersonal Spirit of Naked Being remains.

O

398   When the peace and stillness of pure mind is realised to be the True Nature of the ONE LIFE, then individual consciousness has fallen way to reveal the timeless awareness of THIS.

O

390 THIS is not about being aware, but awareness itself.

O

400 You are free here and now, there is no need to look anywhere, for any act of looking only sustains the illusion that you are presently separated from what you seek. THIS is not about believing *in* something, but embracing and living the essence of who YOU are. What you have been searching for all this time is no other than YOU, for there is no other reality than YOU to find. Even the divine looks out at the mirror of Life through *your* eyes.

O

401 The peace and harmony of THIS does not depend on anything. It is not an experience you have, but an ongoing connection with inner essence.

O

402 THIS consciousness brings about the ending of distinction, the dismantling of separation and leads to Wholeness – Wholeness of Being.

O

403 You never needed to be something, somebody or someone in order to exist, you just needed to allow YOU, BEING, SELF, TRUTH to be consciously present. The Truth of LIFE appears from being YOU in abundance.

O

404   When you are free from any version of who and what you are, YOU are consciously present in the timeless, transpersonal THIS. It's as if you've imagined yourself to have been holding on to a helium filled balloon for years, and in one unexpected instant the balloon is let go. Only then do you discover that you are not the form that was previously holding on to it, but the balloon itself. When the balloon rises to a sufficiently high altitude, it explodes, merging the helium inside the balloon with the totality of the universe. The form of the balloon has disintegrated, but YOU are still present. But where are you? YOU are everywhere and nowhere because YOU are indivisible Spirit – YOU are THIS.

O

405   It is now true to say 'I know nothing' or 'I don't know' because YOU see right through what the 'I' believes itself to be. YOU, on the other hand, do not need to think what YOU are. YOU want for nothing and are separate from nothing, including nothing-ness. So when you are not, YOU absolutely are.

O

406   You are sitting on a chair, inside a house, looking out of a window. Imagine your vision to be pure consciousness, the window to be the mind and the outside to be the physical world of manifested form. Only if the window (the mind) is clear can you truly see through it, for if it is covered in dust and dirt, then the outside view will be difficult or even impossible to make out. So it is with the flow of the Universe. The more you distort pure consciousness with thoughts and beliefs in self, else and

other, then the dirtier the glass and the more misleading the resulting appearance. A clean window creates no illusions, provides no obstructions and projects no ignorance. Likewise, pure mind shines it's lightless light through into the world of form. A complete intelligence beyond the limitations of any individually identified mind. It is for this reason a person who has met and embraced their True Nature is humble and yet empowered, for they have seen their own unimportance and greatness face to face, a sacred timeless occurrence never to be forgotten.

O

407   THIS consciousness will not subside or dissolve. Only perceptions of it will alter. Whether you are born into this world, live in this world or have passed on from this world, THIS awareness will always be. If you are not looking *from or to*, then recognise you are looking *within and through* THIS.

O

408   Even the idea of how you arrived at your understanding of reality is let go. YOU are not to be found 'back there' because YOU are not the experiences. YOU are to be found here and only here. THIS is the only place YOU can be. You are all and nothing. YOU are pure awareness undisturbed by the constant outer motions of life. For when all you *think* you are has been gradually dissolved, then you will see THIS that everyone is.

O

409   If you believe that through the passing of time you have
        moved from A to B and got somewhere, become
        something or are now deserving praise or attention, then
        who is making that assumption and why? You have not
        changed at all because you are the infinite THIS you
        always were. Here, now and always present. You cannot
        alter what THIS is, you may only realise it to be Pure
        Naked Being.

o

410   How beautiful your life is without concepts and ideas.
        Now there is not even the arising of the thought of being
        at one with a tree or a bird, but the natural appearance of
        THIS. There is no thought of oneness, only the living
        reality of what YOU are. By letting go of any separation
        between yourself and *all* other selves, you not only
        perceive THIS – but you realise it to be the transpersonal
        essence of Universal Mind and the Truth of Being.

o

411   Discard everything you have learnt which brought you to
        this point. It was only to bring you here. A comfy chair is
        of little use to you when trying to cross a river.

o

412   Attachment not only applies to form but also to the
        formless.

o

413   When there are no apparent opposites, no being or non-

being, then any doing will be from the spontaneous action of the Self. If you continue to live your life in this way, *all* opposites fall away.

O

414   Awakening balance concerns the elimination of differences. This means arriving at an unwavering acceptance of the relationship between two apparent opposites. Opposites are mutually interdependent measurements, so in fact they are not really different at all. The two poles are then harmonized into the one consistent whole. In the actualisation of Wholeness there is no longer a requirement to label things as good or bad, interior and exterior, self or True Self. When two opposites are recognised to be degrees or variations of the same concept, they become 'fused' together and transcended.

O

415   Experiencing intelligent love simultaneously arises with peace of mind. *Peace of mind* frees the feeling and action of *intelligent love.*

O

416   The perfect beauty and joy of existence appears by simply BEING LIFE.

O

417   To love life and to not love life, being stuck in neither one; this is Wholeness.

O

418 The dual 'you' and non-dual 'YOU' dissolve into HARMONY. Your non-dual based Nature blends back into the duality of the body and the world. A symbiotic relationship arises whereby the pure mind consciousness of THIS acknowledges and works with and through the duality of THAT as a spontaneous unification of inner and outer being occurs. A working relationship between the habitual and pure minds is established. Duality is seen to be the way the physical world functions, but life is lived from the perspective and Self-knowledge of your non-dual Nature.

O

419 From now on you utilise whatever element of being you need in order to carry out the 'job' at hand. You may not require the use of pure mind awareness in order to pay for the groceries, but as the foundation of what YOU are, it will *always* be known to underlie *every* situation, *every* moment. Fully aware but unattached to *any* identity, you act in accordance with the resolution or betterment of any situation, for you are both wise *and* innocent.

O

420 Coming home is not simply the understanding and experiencing of your True Nature, but the actualisation of Wholeness of Being in the world.

O

421 So the truth-seeker arrives at the sought through the

letting go of all concepts of seeking. There is no 'I', no you, no them or us, no self, no True Self, no ONE True Self. On the other hand, it could be equally true to say that they *all* exist. This is the free flowing ocean of LIFE, apparently separate beings sharing the ONE essence of inseparable Being.

O

422 'To be filled is good and to lack is bad. Yet it is also good for you to be lacking but bad for you to be filled. For those who are filled are also lacking and one person who is lacking is not filled in the same way as another. One who is filled, though, becomes sufficiently perfect. Hence you should be lacking when you can be filled and filled when you can be lacking, because then you can be filled even more. So be filled with spirit but lacking in human reason, for human reason is only human reason, and the soul, too, is only soul.' *Jesus of Nazareth* speaking in *The Secret Book of James Ch. 2 v 12-16.* What does this mean to you now? What do you choose to be full of?

O

423 Nothing is sought. What was sought is found. What was found is THIS, the unabridged emptiness of Wholeness. Unlocking any attachment to the seeking of knowledge brings about the ending of assumed identity.

O

424 THIS is Wholeness. THIS is Truth. THIS is Reality. THIS is YOU. Pure mind is the pathway to Wholeness.

O

425   When you realise the Truth of LIFE, difference in all its many guises falls away. The difference between yourself and another, between yourself and a fly, or between yourself and nothing. No difference. Because the fundamental essence of what you are, is the same essence of all things and all non-things. It is the same force, the pure vital energy inherent in the Cosmos. Pure consciousness is pure energy is pure mind.

O

426   Being 'present' is YOU consciously alive within (and inseparable from) the universal ocean of the ONE LIFE. When the wave is known to be in the ocean, and the ocean is known to be in the wave.

O

427   Now you see you have not gained or attained anything. That the habitual mind of duality and the pure mind of non-duality are poles of Being, variations and degrees of the ONE NATURE. As these poles of being are recognised, they are overseen and transcended via the coming together of *all that you are*.

O

428   Duality is the perceived experiencing of subject and object. In non-duality there is no experience to be had as such for there is nobody to experience it and therefore no experience. The overseeing of both poles is Wholeness. Doesn't the act of presently experiencing something make

it real? So what is real is only perceived in accordance with your mind. If you accidentally walk into a coffee table, you will recognise that at a physical level there may be pain, for there is separation. The physical reality of the body is only one level, one layer, one perception of Truth. You cannot physically walk into Truth and yet you can be undeniably aware of its presence. Therefore you can 'see' both. If you can see both form and formlessness without needing to identify yourself with either, then you are FREE.

O

429   You are *a* multi-dimensional being. YOU are multi-dimensional BEING. Both and neither. Not one or the other. For to settle with one ignores the life lesson of human being-ness, that one part needs, while the other needs nothing.

O

430   The way to unify and actualise human being-ness is to understand that the habitual mind of duality is as incomplete as the pure mind of non-duality. For in blending the finite with the infinite, you become the alchemist of the soul, transforming base metal into gold to realise the true elixir of life. You come home to BEING.

O

431   Wholeness is free to be what it is. When you truly recognise that you are both BODY and SPIRIT and the mind clings to *neither*, you transcend the opposing poles of duality and non-duality. For the human being is both Animal and Spirit. If we continue to pursue either our Animal or Spirit Natures alone, without acceptance and

detachment, then both routes will be flawed, for they fail to integrate into Wholeness. What has stopped us from realising this Wholeness has been our continued dependency on opposing poles. The separately identified form of the intelligent Animal pursued the all encompassing indivisible Spirit. It became yet another story of *either – or. Either* we are this *or* we presume to be that. Whereas we are presently both. We are not just the body. We are not simply pure mind alone, or we would have no need for the human body and habitual mind of ego. Becoming Brahman or God-man is not the goal either. It was a signpost, an example. For the human race to survive, develop and continue to grow we must bring our inherent form and formlessness together in order to transcend them. In this way we will realise each one of us to be unique expressions of a unified reality. You are different but not separate. Unique not special. Unusual but amazingly ordinary.

O

432   Recognising existence *and* non-existence is the overseeing way of Wholeness. Giving up both the real and the unreal and continuing a sustained non-reliance on *all* knowledge and occurrences.

O

433   Letting go of our attachments, we find detachment, and in letting go of our detachment, we find Wholeness. When Wholeness is realised, you remain aware of both attachments *and* detachment – *while not identifying with either.*

O

434   When all the modified patterns of the mind are let go, then there remains no dependency or entanglement with ideas such as ignorance or realisation. No comparison remains, for *all life* is seen to be indisputably ONE and the same.

O

435   So consciousness begins as the objective seer, discovers itself to be pure awareness and then realises the overseeing of both elements. In doing so, it actualises Wholeness.

O

436   'The whole is more than the sum of its parts.' Aristotle (384-322 BCE). How can this be so? Logically speaking, the whole should be a combined total of all the parts. Nothing more and nothing less. With consciousness it is more because the mind transcends all versions of separation to arrive at a new perspective, a new overseeing dimension – Wholeness of Being.

O

437   A worldview consciousness which does not place the value or importance of one person, country or religion above another, which does not disseminate the belief in greater and lesser being, presents the most efficient way for life on earth to progress. In this way it remains free to grow while retaining the shared awareness of *all* – allowing the coming into being of a global consciousness which mirrors the creative power of the universe. This is the the way home. The way home to universal intelligence.

O

438   Everything is everything. Everything *is* nothing. Nothing *is*, and everything is. When you leave the 'I' – it fades. When you go beyond 'I AM' – YOU remain. So 'you' won't always exist, but 'YOU' always are. Nothing is absolutely real – only a cover, a disguise for essential BEING. For example, photons are within nuclear particles, which are within atoms, which are within molecules, which are within cells, which are within plants and animals, which are within the living planet, which is part of a solar system, part of a universe and, likewise, part of the entire cosmos. This brings forward some interesting reflections when we see that without photons, or light, we could not exist. You are only here because of LIGHT. We are indeed 'Children of the Light', for we all come from the ONE LIGHT.

O

439   'They address me by different names not realising that they are all the names of the one Tathagata. Some recognise me as Tathagata, some as the Self-existent One, some as Gautama the Ascetic, some as Buddha. Then there are others who recognise me as Brahma, as Vishnu, as Ishvara; some see me as Sun, as Moon; some as a reincarnation of the ancient sages; some as one of 'the ten powers'; some as Rama, some as Indra, and some as Varuna. Still there are others who speak of me as The Un-born, as Emptiness, as 'Such-ness', as Truth, as Reality, as the Ultimate Principle; still there are others who see me as Dharmakaya, as Nirvana, as the Eternal; some speak of me as sameness, as non-duality, as undying, as formless; some think of me as the doctrine of Buddha-causation, or

of Emancipation, or of the Noble Path; and some think of me as Divine Mind and Noble Wisdom. Thus in this world and other worlds am I known by these uncounted names, but they all see me as the moon is seen in the water. Though they all honour, praise and esteem me, they do not fully understand the meaning and significance of the words they use; not having their own self-realisation of Truth, they cling to the words of their canonical books, or to what has been told them, or to what they have imagined, and fail to see that the name they are using is only one of the many names of the Tathagata. In their studies they follow the mere words of the text vainly trying to gain the true meaning, instead of having confidence in the one 'text' where self-confirming Truth is revealed, that is, having confidence in the self-realisation of Noble Wisdom.' So spoke Siddhārtha Gautama (Buddha) as recorded in the Buddhist scripture *The Lankavatara Sutra*. In other words, names and labels are helpful pointers but may also be the cause of ongoing confusion and ignorance. Everything is dogma. If you choose one label, one system, one form, one idea and remain identified with that form rather than allowing yourself to experience your True Nature, then it is just like looking at the reflection of the moon in the water and not touching the reality inside you. The advice here is not to get stuck in the literal meaning of *any* teaching or *any* words but to see for yourself, to investigate truth from within your own being. To BE LIFE. To BE LIGHT. So why not see for yourself what you are? For then you will uncover that YOU are more than Buddha. YOU are more than any name, any label or any word. YOU are the living beyond-ness itself. You are THAT which Buddha was not, and THIS which Buddha IS. YOU are NOW and ALWAYS FREE to BE.

O

440 The many faces are ONE; the numerous appearances derive their apparent uniqueness *from* their absolute unity. Life is the jigsaw puzzle of Being. Each apparently disconnected piece assumes itself to be absolutely different and separate. Only when the pieces are joined together does the full perfect chaos of the picture appear.

O

441 Wholeness goes beyond duality and non-duality because it recognises both the habitual and pure minds to be elements of being human, but neither one to be complete human being-ness. Wholeness recognises the Body - Spirit polarities and remains free from identifying with either. Free to be, free to grow. The habitual mind sees the duality of THAT, pure mind sees the unity of THIS, whereas Wholeness oversees BOTH and so remains open to GROWTH. Accepting Wholeness allows you to be authentic, integrated and FREE. Led by your non-dual essence while remaining aware of the dual nature of the body and the world, your actions escalate the manifestation of pure consciousness. In this way, you remain peacefully grounded yet spontaneously creative, as you realise what it means to be truly WHOLE.

O

442 Sharing the reality of what you are without needing to identify yourself as the doer of the action is your essential Nature.

O

443 Wholeness is arrived at through the acknowledgement and acceptance of *all* outcomes; chaos and perfection, existence and non-existence. It is realised through non-dependence on either attachment or non-attachment.

O

444 Letting go of all modified versions of Truth allows a conscious awareness of its continuous presence, for you cannot remove Truth. When you find *a truth* then let it go, for when you find Truth, it cannot be left.

O

445 What is the universe if not an expression of intelligent organisation? You have the freewill to turn away or to cooperate, just like the bee collecting pollen from the flower. For how long, which flower, when to and when not to, are all manifestations of the freewill of the bee, and yet the underlying process remains intelligently organised. As a human being you have the widest possible choice from freewill and therefore the most profound and sacred responsibility to *all* life.

O

446 You can let go of all 'things' but you cannot let go of essence.

O

447 Essence is pure consciousness is pure energy is Truth. It is not an *object* to be found within ourselves, yet it is found within *all* things. Being, God, Buddha Nature, the Tao, call

it what you will, for this no holds barred everything-ness underlies *all* things. It is the origin of *all* species, the fundamental Nature of who or what everything is.

O

448 Truth is beyond words and letters. To attempt to name and discuss it only creates poor confusing copies of an indescribable reality. What was originally searched for in some type of secret, personal, ego-bound mystery is now seen to be within all things and all non-things. Every thought, occurrence, situation, or form is a manifestation of it. It is the unfathomable, the unmoveable, the undeniable, unabridged awareness brought about through the undoing of thought and form.

O

449 The human struggle is a search for Wholeness. We spend our lives trying to be complete. We begin by accumulating as much material wealth, status, power, honour and conditioned versions of 'success' as we possibly can, but in the end all of these are found to be lacking. None of them can be sustained, for they are mind made creations. We realise that the meaning we seek is never going to be found outside of ourselves, and so we begin to search inside. When we delve deeply into our core, we find that our inner being is mystifyingly empty – empty of self. Within this emptiness, the fullness of LIFE is uncovered. From this non-dual awakening we see all 'things' as illusory because the world of form is recognised to be fleeting and in a sense 'unreal'. As awareness deepens, a real grounding and balancing of the poles of being occurs. The non-dual Spirit becomes established in the duality of

the body and the world, providing a practical way for Naked Being to manifest. A rounded Wholeness arises from accepting the outer self to be the way your non-dual Nature is released into the world. You now know yourself to be a unique individual following the ONE essence of LIFE called Spirit.

O

450 When we take a walk in the countryside and hear it in the sweet song of the birds – when we see it in the multi-coloured pebbles and restless green weeds of the flowing stream – when we discover it in the gnarled base of a rotten oak tree, sense it in the invisible air we breathe and feel its warm embrace as the sunlight touches our face – when we go through the towns and cities and hear it in the never-ending noise and see it written plainly in the eyes and on the faces of *all* people – then there is nothing more to say than *THIS is in all to BE, for Naked Being is within ALL to see.*

THE END

Notes and Recommended Resources

Marvin.W.Meyer (Trans). *The Secret Teachings of Jesus: Four Gnostic Gospels* (Random House, 1984) pp.123, 422

Coleman Banks (Trans). *Rumi, Selected Poems* (Penguin Books, 1995) p.345

Gangaji. *The Diamond in Your Pocket* (Sounds True, 2007)

Jean Klein. *Be Who You Are* (Non-duality Press, 2006)

Eckhart Tolle. *The Power of Now: A Guide to Spiritual Enlightenment* (New World Library, 1999)

Eckhart Tolle *Stillness Speaks* (New World Library, 2003)

Eckhart Tolle. *A New Earth: Awakening to your life's purpose* (Penguin, 2005)

Ramana Maharshi. *Be As You Are: The Teachings of Sri Raman Maharshi,* edited by David Godman (Arkana, 1985)

Dennis Gempel Merzel. *Big Mind - Big Heart: Finding Your Way* (Big Mind Publishing, 2007)

Khenchen Thrangu Rinpoche. *Essentials of Mahamudra: Looking Directly at the Mind* (Wisdom Publications, 2004)

Sri Nisargadatta. *I Am That,* (Acorn Press, 1990)

Jerry Katz. *One: Essential Writings on Nonduality.* (Sentient Publications, 2007)

Anthony De Mello. *Awareness* (Image, 1990)

Paul Brunton. *Advanced Contemplation The Peace Within You, Vol. 15: Notebooks of Paul Brunton* (Larson Publications, 1988)

Nouk Sanchez and Tomas Vieira. *Take Me To The Truth* (O books, 2007)

H.W.L.Poonja. *Wake Up and Roar: Satsang With H.W.L.Poonja, Vol. 1* (Gangaji Foundation, 1992)

www.forgottenbooks.org is a great site for finding ancient wisdom material such as *A Buddhist Bible, The Dhammapada, The Bhagavad-Gita, The Tao* and many more.

Further Info

If you would like to ask a question or comment on *Naked Being*, find out about talks, workshops, retreats and personal sessions with Jonathan (J.M.Harrison) then visit:

www.wholenessofbeing.com

B O O K S

O is a symbol of the world, of oneness and unity. In different cultures it also means the "eye," symbolizing knowledge and insight. We aim to publish books that are accessible, constructive and that challenge accepted opinion, both that of academia and the "moral majority."

Our books are available in all good English language bookstores worldwide. If you don't see the book on the shelves ask the bookstore to order it for you, quoting the ISBN number and title. Alternatively you can order online (all major online retail sites carry our titles) or contact the distributor in the relevant country, listed on the copyright page.

See our website **www.o-books.net** for a full list of over 500 titles, growing by 100 a year.

And tune in to myspiritradio.com for our book review radio show, hosted by June-Elleni Laine, where you can listen to the authors discussing their books.

MySpiritRadio